THE PHOTOGRAPHIC

I CHING

From Christine

Dec 1998

THE PHOTOGRAPHIC
I CHING

Photographs by
GARY WOODS

A new interpretation by
DHIRESHA MCCARVER

based on the translation by James Legge

Marlowe & Company

THE PHOTOGRAPHIC I CHING

Copyright © 1996 Labyrinth Publishing (UK) Ltd.
Photographs © 1996 Gary Woods.

The rights of Gary Woods to be identified as the photographer and Dhiresha McCarver
to be identified as the author of the work have been asserted by them in accordance with the
Copyright, Design and Patents Act, 1988.

Manufactured in Italy

FIRST MARLOWE & COMPANY EDITION, 1997

Published in the United States of America by
Marlowe & Company
632 Broadway, Seventh Floor
New York, NY 10012

THE PHOTOGRAPHIC I CHING was produced by Labyrinth Publishing (UK) Ltd
Design & art direction by Richard Adams Associates
Typesetting by Wayzgoose

Library of Congress Cataloging-in-Publication Data on this title is
available on request from the publisher.

ISBN 1-56924-773-0

CONTENTS

INTRODUCTION

THE *I CHING*, or "Book of Changes," was compiled from earlier sources by Confucian philosophers during the Chou Dynasty, about two and a half thousand years ago. This ancient oracle, originally involving the use of bones, and later the stalks of the yarrow plant, has become, without doubt, one of the most profound and revealing devices. The system of sixty-four hexagrams, showing permutations of yin and yang lines, gives insights which help release the transformative energies of the questioner. Each hexagram is composed of two trigrams, which represent the natural phenomena, such as heaven, thunder, water, as in clouds, or as collected in a lake, mountain, earth, wind or wood, and fire. Each of these elements also symbolizes certain aspects of human nature, which combined give the interpretation of the hexagram.

The ancient Chinese view of life attaches meaning to all life forces; however, the very absence of meaning given to chance eventually allowed its use to express a deeper significance. The concept of an oracle is a refinement of this idea. Chinese characters are developments of early pictograms, and the interplay between image and text is one of the original features of the *I Ching*. The fraction of time needed to expose a photograph may parallel the act of throwing dice or tossing coins. A photograph, like a hexagram, results from the coincidence of chance elements observed at a particular moment.

The photographs in this edition attempt to reflect the natural phenomena indicated by the trigrams or to make some association with the title of the hexagram.

The *I Ching* not only speaks to us about our present situation but resolves enquiries as to the nature of our destinies. This poetic and mature work has informed much of China's philosophy, religion and poetry, and is as much a book of ideas as it is an oracular text. As such, I would like to suggest that before making any consultations of a divinatory nature you take the opportunity to read the text all the way through. This will familiarize those who may be new to the *I Ching* with the continuity underlying the order in which the hexagrams are presented.

It has been our intention, in *The Photographic I Ching*, to make the spirit of this ancient document available on many different levels. This edition has been based upon the earliest English translation of the *I Ching*, that of James Legge (1815–97), who was the first professor of Chinese at Oxford University, and I have taken the conscious decision to write my interpretations in a form which reflects Legge's translation as closely as possible. I have, however, taken a few liberties with the language; for example, I have introduced the term "socio-political" to encompass all areas of personal relationships, and to minimize some of the more class-related distinctions found in the original text. I have generally referred to the "superior person" rather than to Legge's "superior man," but have chosen to retain the masculine pronouns throughout the text simply to maintain an uninterrupted flow for the reader. The wisdom of the *I Ching* is not restricted by gender. It is universal; so too are the words and images used to express it.

Dhiresha McCarver
London 1996

HEAVEN *the creative*

HEAVEN is the symbol of firmness, the primal yang nature. Comprised of six undivided lines, this hexagram doubles the trigram heaven; thus we have heaven above and heaven below. Heaven, in its motion, indicates strength. It represents what is great and originating, penetrating, advantageous, correct and firm. It is the symbol of renewed, untiring effort. The superior person devotes himself to ceaseless activity in both spiritual and physical endeavors, creating peace, security and union for all.

The image is of heaven moving with unceasing power, reflected in the strong and untiring superior person.

THE LINES

1 | The time is not yet ripe for the power to be manifested. It is not the time for active doing. The calm strength of patience will be of great benefit.

2 | The creative power begins to be felt. This is the time to seek counsel from wise and experienced people, not the time to act without guidance.

3 | Here we see the vigilant actions of the superior person begin to bring recognition. Now it is essential to balance the outward actions by moral stability. The situation is dangerous, but through careful consideration there will be no mistake.

4 | The moment of choice has come—to go forward or to withdraw into solitude. The decision must be in complete accord with one's innermost being. There is no universal right or wrong.

5 | As the power is now fully unfurled, it will be advantageous to meet with the great one. Like energies align themselves with one another. Seek only the companionship of those of a similar nature.

6 | If the creative power exceeds its proper limits there will undoubtedly be cause for repentance. The law of nature states that what is too full must be emptied. Isolation is the result of unrestrained display of power.

EARTH *the receptive*

EARTH is the symbol of submission, the primal yin nature. This hexagram is made up of six divided lines. Doubling the trigram earth gives us earth above and earth below. The strength of earth lies in quietness and firmness; the major attribute is perseverance. The docile devotion of earth forms the perfect complement to the ceaseless activity of heaven. In no way are these two hexagrams seen to be in opposition to one another. They are, rather, the ultimate expressions of the two primal forces evident in all forms of human experience. The creative (heaven) initiates ideas, and the receptive (earth) gives them form. It is in the nature of earth to follow. When the superior person needs to make some movement, it is best not to take the initiative, but to follow the guiding influences with devotion. Advantages will come from seeking friendships where your effort and work will be recognized, forgoing those liaisons that involve planning with others. Perpetually rest in correctness and firmness, and there will be good fortune.

The image is one of the tireless mare, strong and devoted in her service to mankind. She is yielding, yet quietly powerful in the fulfillment of her duty.

THE LINES

1 | Beware the appearance of hoar frost, which indicates the beginnings of evil. Left unexposed, evil will become as thick and solid as ice, leading to misfortune. Pay careful attention to any signs of decay.

2 | The receptive, yielding to the creative, follows the harmonious flow and produces good results without effort. Trust in the rightness of your actions. This is not the time to doubt. Be dutiful, consistent and true.

3 | Much can be accomplished without drawing attention to oneself. If a person must be of service at this time, he should retain as low a profile as possible. Any efforts undertaken now will bring good results for future development.

4 | This is a dangerous period, where caution and reserve are indicated in all matters. Hiding oneself will bring no cause for either blame or praise.

5 | This is the time for utmost discretion. Good fortune is certainly at hand, but must be received with great humility.

6 | The surest way to destroy all that has been gained is to create opposition between the natural forces of yin and yang. Both sides will be hurt.

INITIAL DIFFICULTIES

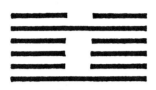

INITIAL DIFFICULTIES is the symbol of bursting. The trigram water positioned over that of thunder indicates profound movement. It is in the positioning of the trigrams that we find release from the difficult beginning. The natural movement of water is downward; that of thunder (arousing) is upward. When the two meet, the resulting thunderstorm clears the air. The times are full of difficulties and chaos, but perseverance in the beginning will result in long-lasting success. Advantages will come from being correct and firm. Any premature action will certainly bring disaster. Great patience is needed. The present condition is one of disorder, a state which often precedes great revolutions. The superior person will use the initial period to gather supportive helpers. This is not the time to remain alone. Many people and situations will present themselves. Take care to sort out only the best ingredients from all that is available. Sorting the threads from what, at first, appears to be a big tangle, before beginning to weave, is truly a difficult task.

The image is of a plant, struggling with difficulty in its transformation from a seed, rising gradually above the surface of the earth towards the sky.

THE LINES

1 | This is not the time to advance. It is much more advantageous to use the time to seek out willing helpers. To do this, one must remain free from arrogance, reflecting at all times on the worthiness of the goal.

2 | Beware the appearance of a quick solution to difficulties. The result could certainly be a shock. It is better to remain correct and firm than to enter into an arrangement that will limit your freedom. More time is needed.

3 | To proceed without proper guidance at this stage will be disastrous. It may mean relinquishing what at first appears to be a profitable venture, in order to avoid disgrace.

4 | The time has come to accept the offer of help from one who is in a position to offer it. Joining forces at this time is advantageous, even if it initially feels uncomfortable. Success is indicated.

5 | Misunderstandings of good intentions can best be avoided by proceeding with the utmost caution. Do not try to force anything. The best rewards will be found in small measures, not great ones.

6 | Not every seed sprouts. If the difficulties cannot be overcome, accept this and start afresh.

YOUTHFUL INEXPERIENCE

YOUTHFUL INEXPERIENCE is the symbol of obscurity. The trigram mountain, resting as it naturally does over water, indicates that there will be progress and success. The hexagram speaks to both the seeker and the sought. Inexperience is not to be misinterpreted as ignorance or stupidity. It is nothing more than lack of experience. The way to increase understanding, and transform immaturity into enlightenment, is humbly to seek a wizened teacher. The teacher does not overtly seek the student. If the student approaches with sincerity and respect, great benefit will come from the meeting. Receptivity in the beginning must not be allowed to disintegrate into youthful immaturity, or the teacher will undoubtedly lose patience with the pupil. The wise teacher will not expend the energy to instruct the troublesome, and foolish questioning will be met with silence, if not punishment. There will be advantage in remaining correct and firm. Success will come only through steadfast perseverance, with the will of the student responding with respect to the will of the teacher. The superior person will seize the opportunity to nourish virtue, be it that of student or teacher, and not use the occasion to draw attention to himself.

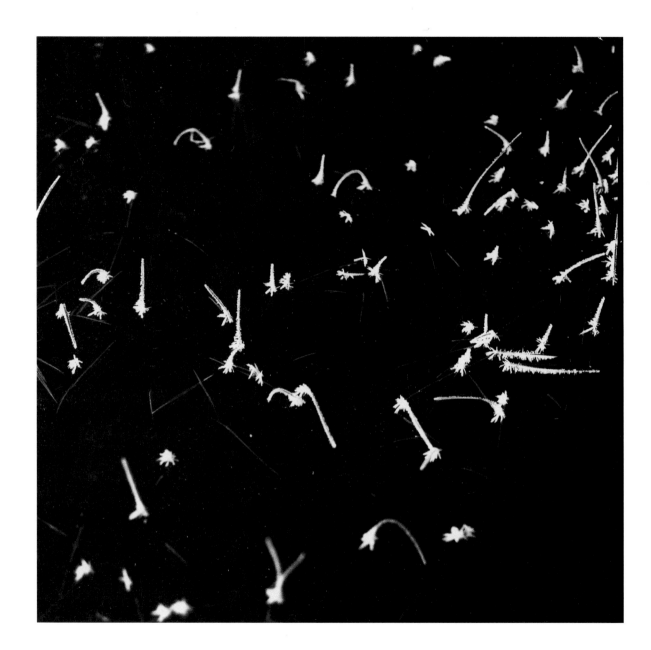

The image is of a clear mountain stream, flowing to bring life to all the small plants now struggling forth at the base of the mountain.

THE LINES

1 | Correct discipline, administered wisely, will help to dispel ignorance. Indiscriminately imposed discipline creates weak individuals, and will bring cause for regret.

2 | There will be good fortune if one maintains the qualities of kindness and responsibility when dealing with the inexperienced. It may be necessary to sustain the weaker members of the team for a while. Harmony will result.

3 | It will be disastrous to align oneself with anyone who is too much attached to wealth or fame. Maintain dignity by remaining correct and firm.

4 | It is better to withdraw from a truly ignorant person than to remain by his side out of a sense of duty. Humiliation is unavoidable in such a situation.

5 | Innocence is rewarded. One who approaches the teacher with an open heart, without arrogance, will experience good fortune.

6 | When a person must administer punishment, he should take care not to use violence. The purpose of punishment is to restore order, not to destroy the individual.

DELAYING

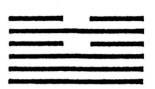

DELAYING is expressed in the symbol of waiting. The trigram water (peril) positioned over that of heaven (strength) indicates full rain clouds accumulating in the sky. Strength, confronted by peril, could make the mistake of rising prematurely to confront it. The superior person knows the folly of encountering danger before the time is ripe. Well-considered actions and carefully matured plans will bring brilliant success. One must patiently wait, even in the face of imminent danger, for the appropriate time to act. Firm correctness will be needed when undertaking hazardous enterprises or encountering great difficulties; but the end result will be advantageous for the one who waits with awareness. One is advised to enjoy the time of delayed activity by nourishing oneself with good food and drink. The ability to see things exactly as they are, without illusion, will be of tremendous help during this period of waiting. Going forward at the appropriate time will be followed by meritorious achievement.

The image is of the rain cloud, filled to capacity, releasing its nourishment on all things that grow.

THE LINES

1 | There is danger in the air. Be aware of it, yet make no movement to encounter it. Maintain an orderly existence in order to remain free from error or blame.

2 | The danger draws near. The small injury of being spoken against by others is best met with restraint. Generosity now will result in good fortune.

3 | The danger is at hand. One invites injury by not heeding the advice against advancing. Be cautious in your relationships with others.

4 | Waiting, even in face of utmost danger, is the only solution. Prudent measures are indicated. One must accommodate the situation, and escape as soon as possible.

5 | Patience is rewarded. Enjoy the food and drink with good cheer. Remain correct and firm, and further good fortune will follow.

6 | One is totally surrounded by danger. There is no way to avoid it any longer. Yield gracefully. This will bring unexpected help which, if treated respectfully, will dispel the danger.

CONFLICT

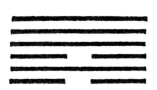

CONFLICT is represented by the symbol of contention. The trigram heaven, with its tendency to move upward, is positioned over that of water, with its tendency to move downward. Hence we see a new interaction between heaven and water. Strength without peril would not produce contention; peril without strength would not be able to contend. It is the coming together of strength and peril that denotes conflict. This can be expressed in the sense of conflict between what one considers to be the inner nature of being and the outer, external forces. The element of sincerity is introduced into the hexagram, to remind us that even though a person may be sincere in his cause, conflict in itself is damaging, and to be avoided whenever possible. Conflict springs from egoism, and, once initiated, will continue to meet with opposition and obstructions to feed its development. If a person maintains an apprehensive caution in contentious situations, there will be good results. If, however, he insists on prosecuting the contention to the bitter end, there will be disaster. The superior person recognizes the benefits of seeking inspired counsel, and will not attempt to take on hazardous enterprises unsupported.

The image is one of heaven and water going their separate ways with great show of force.

1 | The conflict has already arisen. Do not perpetrate it. Be prepared to suffer the small injury of being spoken against. The end result is fortunate.

2 | When faced with conflict, especially if the opponent has superior strength, retreat at once. Do not attempt to draw others into the conflict on your behalf. To engage in such activity would invite calamity.

3 | Remain correct and firm. Withdraw completely from any cause of conflict. Do not commit yourself to projects with the intent of gaining rewards. Keep to the background, and good fortune will result.

4 | Returning to the study of what is right in principle will result in abandoning the desire for conflict. This is the course which will lead to good fortune.

5 | The only way to truly resolve conflict is to trust the matter to one who has unobstructed vision. Great good fortune will come to the one who is judged to be in the right.

6 | Carrying conflict to the bitter end may result in temporary rewards, but persistence in such behavior is sure to end in defeat and disgrace.

GROUP ACTION

GROUP ACTION is the symbol of multitude. With the trigram earth (docility) positioned over that of water (danger), it indicates how a leader of appropriate age and experience, who acts with firmness and correctness, will bring good fortune and not error. The hexagram refers specifically to any undertakings that require a strong rule. The superior person, in accordance with this, nourishes and educates all of the people, in order to gather from them the ones needed to carry out the campaign. A sense of trust and common values must prevail if people are to engage in any activity together. The "rules" are twofold: the objective of the expedition must be righteous in itself; and the manner of conducting it, especially at the outset, must also be right. The superior person is well aware that the powers invested in him are solely for the benefit of the whole group. There must be one ruling will and mind; a divided authority is sure to fail. Therefore, it is with the utmost respect and compassion that a superior person takes on this role. People will endure and accomplish much on behalf of a leader whom they truly esteem and love. Moral correctness must pervade all undertakings.

The image is of water being held in place by the governing body of the earth, as in a very deep well.

THE LINES

1 | This is the time to begin new projects. If all objectives are deemed to be true and right, success will follow. If not, there will certainly be cause for regret.

2 | The leader who works within the group will bring good fortune for all. His appointment has been well considered from many other contenders. No error will mar his undertakings.

3 | Leadership must remain intact. Inefficient people may attempt to put themselves forward. To follow such fools will bring cause for regret.

4 | The superior person knows when to retreat. To advance when the time is not right leads to disaster. Better to organize a skillful retreat and wait for more fortunate circumstances. There is no evidence of failure in retreat.

5 | In no circumstances should the young and inexperienced assume positions of power. They are not yet ready to share the command. Their presence can overshadow even the most well-placed leader, bringing misfortune to all.

6 | Everyone will share in the profits of victory. The superior person must divide the rewards carefully. Do not place inferior people in positions where the welfare of others will depend on them.

UNION

UNION is the symbol of collaboration. The trigram water, positioned over that of earth, represents a natural correctness. Water upon the surface of the earth will form itself into rivers and streams. The wise ruler will use this principle to ensure that all members of the union are held together out of trust and mutual respect. The central figure must be willing to examine his character carefully, to determine that he has the strength of virtue to fulfill the task of leader. If he finds that he does not, he must depart at once, for the very nature of union requires a strong center. If these conditions are met, good fortune will result. The implication of "help" is apparent in the relationships between the members of the union, and in their genuine devotion to the worthy leader. The people who choose to form this union will do so out of their shared commitment to the harmony of the group. The individuals will recognize their own interests reflected in the workings of the group. Not all will be able to commit themselves readily to such a union; those who hesitate too long in making their decision will experience regret.

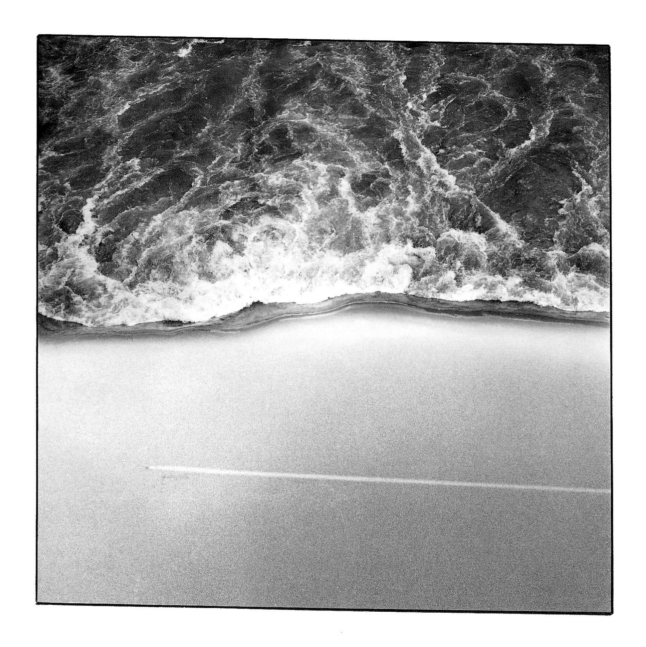

The image is of water flowing naturally into rivers and streams, formed by the powerful nature of the earth.

THE LINES

1 | Unions based on sincerity will prosper. The union itself is like an earthenware vessel, containing the proceeds of the works of the members.

2 | The movement towards union arises from one's innermost convictions; not from persuasion by others.

3 | Make sure that union is sought only with the right people, and not out of desperation.

4 | Once one has committed oneself to the union, wholehearted participation will bring rewards.

5 | When the leader is justly placed, people will seek to find union with others who are also attracted by his virtue. No one is solicited, nor is anyone forced to remain.

6 | Without commitment to the union there can be no progress. The time for hesitation has passed.

MINOR RESTRAINT

MINOR RESTRAINT is the symbol of the taming force of gentleness. The trigram wind, blowing over that of heaven, creates great clouds—but no rain. The restraint can only be minor. The natural force of nature will require the clouds to release the rain when the time is right. Without the gentle force of the wind, the clouds would not be able to gather themselves together. Therefore, the restraint is viewed as a positive force, indicating the progress and success to come. The promise of rain is in the air. The shadow of the clouds are felt on the earth below. All things are waiting to spring to life; yet the gentle winds continue to blow the clouds around. The wise man will follow the example of the cloud, and maintain his inner strength while displaying outward flexibility. This time is well spent in developing one's inner skills, and then manifesting them outwardly in everyday actions. It is not time to change the world by forceful measures. There are still obstacles to be overcome, and the best way to do this will be through gentle persuasion. The restraint is not long lasting. With firm determination, the rain will come.

The image is of laden rain clouds, being prevented from unleashing their full stores by the gentle winds that continue to blow them about.

THE LINES

1 | Good fortune will result from returning to oneself and pursuing a familiar course of action. The obstacles are present to prevent one from foolishly attempting to use force where none is necessary.

2 | Others have also felt the restraint. Join forces with like-minded friends rather than trying to move forward alone.

3 | One is deceived by the gentleness of the restraint, and mistakenly attempts to move forward. The result is disastrous, and even one's friends and family will find it difficult to forgive such behavior.

4 | To avoid mistakes, one must be willing to accept harsh truths and to influence others to do the same. Danger can be averted, and sincerity will be rewarded.

5 | Those who are joined together in sincerity and truthfulness will enjoy the benefits of enduring friendship. Shared resources result in richness for all.

6 | The rain has fallen. To press for more at this time is ill advised.

TREADING CAREFULLY

TREADING CAREFULLY is the symbol of deliberate action. With the trigram heaven positioned over that of water, we have the element of weakness, treading ever so lightly upon that of strength. The hexagram is named from an old Chinese expression about "treading on a tiger's tail." This was a way of describing any activity that was considered to be hazardous. Another attribute of treading carefully is that of pleased perfection. One must tread with utmost caution, paying particular attention to all the rules of good behavior, if one is not to end up in the jaws of the tiger. When one's conduct reflects an observance of the rules of courtesy, then one may proceed to tread safely, even amid scenes of danger and disorder. It is as well to remember that even difficult people respond well to pleasant manners. The pleasure and satisfaction that a person derives from successfully completing a dangerous task must not be allowed to inflate his sense of self pride. It is mostly due to the lightness of his touch that the tiger has agreed not to bite him. Harmonious behavior will be rewarded by progress and success.

The image is of heaven rising high above the lake to assume its natural position; thus even the careful tread of a lesser person will be received with good humor.

THE LINES

1 | One will progress by treading one's accustomed path. Inner strength and simplicity will be rewarded.

2 | Good fortune will come to the quiet and solitary person who treads his path without being distracted from its level and easy way. Remain correct and firm.

3 | Ill fortune is in store for the one who disregards his natural limitations, and treads unconsciously on the tail of the tiger. He will be bitten.

4 | The combination of inner power and outer caution will enable one to tread safely on the tail of the tiger.

5 | Remain aware of the danger. It does not go away, even though your efforts are correct and firm.

6 | Reflect on the course that you have taken. If your actions have been complete and without failure, there will be great good fortune. Congratulations are in order.

PEACE

PEACE is the symbol of success. The trigrams heaven and earth are correctly positioned in their natural order. As it is the nature of heaven (the creative) to rise, and of earth (the receptive) to descend, their union will bring good fortune, with progress and success. Harmonious conditions are the result of the communication between heaven and earth. Peace indicates the first month of the natural spring, when the nourishing effects of the sun and genial skies are most profoundly felt. The process of growth is manifest everywhere. Peace also harmonizes the relationships between men. Just as the breath of spring calls forth all plant life, affairs of mankind must also be conducted in accord with the laws of nature. This time of social harmony is the result of diligent effort by all the members, each following instinctively his own inner voice. The success that is inherent in peace must never be taken for granted. All things ebb and flow with the seasons, making this the time to put special effort into all endeavors, so that their benefits may be reaped throughout the year.

The image is of the unity of heaven and earth that brings forth peace and prosperity.

1 | When the time is right to move forward, the wise man will find like-minded people drawn to him. His movement will be supported by the others, and bring success.

2 | Good fortune will follow when one conducts oneself with compassion toward all living things. Find the middle way.

3 | All things will change. But through continued right actions, the success enjoyed today will continue for a long time.

4 | Spontaneous meetings with others will enhance the prospects of continuing success.

5 | The union of heaven and earth is modest and sincere. He who conducts himself accordingly will benefit.

6 | When disorder is apparent, retreat without regret. It is not the time to fight; let events take their course.

RETROGRESSION

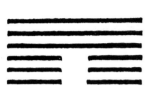

RETROGRESSION is symbolized by stagnation. With the trigram heaven situated above that of earth, we see the exact opposite of the previous hexagram, Peace. Here the creative force of heaven pulls further and further away from the receptive earth, which is sinking into decay. The two elements are estranged from each other. There is no communication between them. The wise man recognizes this as the seventh month of the natural season. The genial forces have done their work, and the processes of growth are at an end. Autumnal decay is an integral part of the life cycle, when all living things experience a season of stagnation. This is not a permanent condition, and the time is most advantageously used to draw oneself into seclusion and reflect upon the nature of decay. In social conditions, the retrogression is brought about when inferior people have advanced to positions of self-importance. Confusion and disorder will result. When one is no longer able to exert a positive influence, it is better to restrain one's actions altogether, and thus avoid the misfortunes that threaten the situation. Involvement with unscrupulous people will surely lead to regret. Accepting the retrogression, and drawing inward, one will develop the inner strength needed to remain unaffected.

The image is of heaven pulling away from the earth and allowing all things to stagnate.

1 | Reject the tendency to be drawn into the disorder for any reason. Choose friends carefully. Avoid humiliation by withdrawing inward.

2 | The attributes of patience and correctness will help one to avoid the disorder. There is no need to become defensive; a quiet and humble manner will bring success.

3 | Inferior people will not be able to maintain control. Their shame signals a turning-point.

4 | Now is the time to act with integrity. Bold action, taken with authority, will result in success and happiness. Like-minded people will share the benefits.

5 | Great strength and virtue are needed to bring the disorder to a close. Respect the fear that arises—its absence could lead to complacency.

6 | There is an end to the condition of stagnation, and the consequences will be expressed in joy.

COMPANIONSHIP

COMPANIONSHIP is the symbol of community. Here we see another complementary alignment of the trigrams, with heaven positioned over that of fire. The natural tendency of fire is to rise and join with the sky, a motion which is in harmony with the idea of union. Companionship represents a condition of nature opposite to that of Retrogression. There was distress and obstruction; here is union. But the union must be based on public considerations and free from all selfish motives. As the sun shines on all equally, so will true companionship among men be based on concerns that are universal. The resultant communities will arise from the shared goals for humanity, and not from the private interests of individuals. When such unity prevails, even dangerous tasks can be undertaken. The wise man will recognize the diversity among men, reflected in the contrasting elements of heaven and fire. Though different by nature, they move in the same direction. Inner clarity will give the strength to cope with the greatest of difficulties and to organize the communities for the benefit of all.

The image is of fire, manifest in the rising sun, which joyfully and spontaneously blazes into the sky to shed its light on everyone.

THE LINES

1 | When people gather freely and openly, without the taint of selfishness, there will be no error.

2 | Relationships based on exclusive principles will degenerate into petty bickering and bring cause for regret.

3 | When a person mistrusts the other members of the community, he will find himself more and more alienated from it. The faults that one perceives in others are often found to be present in oneself.

4 | When reconciliation comes after a quarrel, there will be good fortune.

5 | People who are unified in their innermost hearts will wail and cry out against the obstacles that separate them, and laugh when they are dissolved.

6 | Unions formed on the mere chance of location may lack the warmth of attachment that springs from the heart, but there will be no cause for repentance.

GREAT POSSESSION

GREAT POSSESSION is the symbol of abundance. The position of the trigram fire over that of heaven depicts a fire above the sky that will shine far. The vastness of this light reflects the prosperity and abundance that are indicated when one has the sensibility to remain humble. The combination of the inner strength of heaven with that of the outer clarity of fire will surely produce a person of great inner wealth. There may also be an outer wealth of a material nature, but it is the inner wealth that confers on one the position of authority. The danger that threatens such a position stems from the pride that could arise. So long as one remains unselfish, modest and kind, the danger will be averted and there will be great progress and success. People will be attracted by the power that expresses itself in a graceful and controlled way; thus the wise man will find himself surrounded by strong and willing helpers. One will do well to remember that the light of the sun exposes both good and evil. By extinguishing what is evil, one gives distinction to what is good, in accordance with the will of heaven which has given all men a nature that is fitted for goodness.

The image is of the elegance and brightness of the sun, whose light shines with strength and vigor on all things.

THE LINES

1 | If one recognizes the difficulties and danger of the situation, and avoids arrogance, there will be no error.

2 | The virtue that has been accumulated can be distributed among able helpers without fear of mistake.

3 | The wise man makes his wealth available to the king; the inferior man becomes arrogant.

4 | There is no error in keeping one's resources under restraint.

5 | Sincerity and dignity will be appreciated. Good fortune will come through proper conduct.

6 | The influences of heaven are felt by one who remains modest, even in the face of great reward.

MODESTY

MODESTY is the symbol of humbleness. The trigram earth being positioned over that of the mountain indicates a rising of the heavenly principle of humbleness. The hexagram rightly follows the preceding one of Great Possession, in reminding us that humility is the way to permanent success. The strong mountain humbly gathers the benefits of heaven, and dispenses them to all things through the resulting rain showers. The wise man, in accordance with this humbleness, will be able to deal with all things evenly according to the nature of each. In whatever circumstances or place he finds himself, he will inevitably do what is right. The mountain rising in the midst of the earth follows the same natural law that governs the cycles of the sun and moon. The way to expansion is through contraction. Just as it is the way of heaven for the sun to decline after reaching its zenith, and the moon to wane after it is full, the superior person will diminish what is excessive in himself, and strive to increase the goodness in areas where there is any defect. Modesty is the foundation for sincere moral conduct. Through one's conduct, one draws to oneself the effects of positive or negative influences. It is the way of mankind to hate arrogance and to love the modest. Modesty wins love. Humbleness in a position of power will give cause for the light to shine even more brightly, resulting in a creative display of beauty and fertility on earth.

The image is of a receptive earth, lying low and receiving the blessings from heaven, which give rise to the great mountain that springs forth from her depths.

THE LINES

1 | Modesty nourishes virtue. Even dangerous and difficult tasks can be undertaken when attended to directly and simply.

2 | One's inner nature is reflected in outward modesty. Remain firm and correct, and others will be influenced.

3 | Avoid difficulties by remaining modest, even when accomplishments have been great. Love and support from others are forthcoming.

4 | Take great care not to use false modesty as an excuse to decline responsibility. This is the time to act, taking full account of others.

5 | In extreme situations one may be forced to employ severe measures. Modest conduct will attract rich and powerful supporters.

6 | Modesty is expressed in self-discipline. Act only to assert what is right; and then only within one's own set of circumstances.

HARMONIOUS JOY

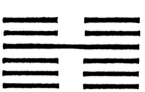

HARMONIOUS JOY is the symbol of enthusiasm. The trigram thunder issues forth from the earth with a crash. The resultant thunderstorm clears the air, and removes all feelings of oppression that may have previously been felt. The condition is one of harmony, happy contentment and satisfaction. Harmonious Joy is the product of devotion within and movement without. The arousal of thunder indicates a time of intense creativity and enthusiasm. The superior person is met with joyful obedience from his subjects, when he adjusts himself to the character of those who are led. The harmonious laws of movement that determine the orbits of celestial bodies and the rhythmical seasons of nature are the same as those that regulate the events of human life. As heaven and earth move with devotion, so too will people rejoice and readily submit to a kind and generous ruler. When such circumstances prevail, any undertakings will be hailed and supported. The threat of opposition is removed, and all people can move forward with enthusiasm. The powerful sound of crashing thunder reduces tension, and reminds one of the music that is composed for sacred ceremonies. The joy and relief expressed through song and dance are a physical manifestation of one's inner devotion.

The image is of the arousing power of a thunderstorm that clears the air and generates a sense of enthusiasm for all things to flourish.

THE LINES

1 | Enthusiasm that boasts, or becomes arrogant, will bring misfortune. Be modest in expression.

2 | Avoid being swept along in the illusions of others. Great clarity is needed, and is rewarded with good fortune.

3 | Looking elsewhere for rewards while indulging one's sense of satisfaction will bring cause for repentance. Be self-reliant, and do not hesitate.

4 | When one's actions are sincere and free from suspicion, friends will gather with enthusiasm and support.

5 | Chronic complaints obstruct enthusiasm, and prevent one from breathing freely. The central danger is of being carried away by the lust of pleasure.

6 | One who is deluded by false enthusiasm will experience much difficulty. But great are the rewards for one who corrects the error.

FOLLOWING

FOLLOWING is the symbol of succession. The strong trigram of thunder, being positioned under that of water, indicates the joy in movement that induces following. By accepting subordination to the weak, the strong defers to the weak and shows consideration, thus giving cause for the follower to be joyful. In succeeding the hexagram of Harmonious Joy, signifying harmony and satisfaction, we see that when these conditions are prevalent people are sure to follow. They will not be coerced into following anyone with whom they do not share a sense of general wellbeing. The hexagram addresses the flexible circumstances in which a person may be the one who is following others, or the one who is being followed. Great progress and success are indicated in both situations, when the follower is guided by a reference to what is proper and correct. Only when this condition of rightness is fulfilled can a person ask others to follow him. The same reference is applied to conditions under which one may successfully follow others without coming to harm. Following is based on the willing adherence of the members. Anything that attempts to undermine this cohesion, such as the use of force or creation of divided factions, will give rise to resistance, and decay will follow. The hexagram also points to a broader sense of following by adapting to

the demands of time. The superior person recognizes the need for rest and recuperation, and draws himself inward to relax. The energy spent in mistaken resistance will not correct a faulty situation.

The image is of thunder being drawn in upon itself. The ripples on the water reflect a following movement, adapting to the time.

THE LINES

1 | It is natural to change the object of one's pursuit. By mixing with people of differing views, one will be able to discern what is right.

2 | When a person chooses to remain with the inferior, he cuts himself off from the influence of the superior. It is not possible to have both at the same time.

3 | Careful choices will be rewarded. Adhere to what is correct and firm, and allow the superficial to fall away.

4 | Beware the following of those who flatter. Sincerely pursue your course with intelligence, to avoid misfortune.

5 | When a person's position is guided by what is correct and true, he will foster what is excellent in others, and good fortune will result.

6 | Even one who has drawn away to rest will respond to a sincere call to further what is right.

DECAYING

DECAYING is the symbol of major power. The attribute of the mountain, stoppage or arrest, positioned over the pliancy of wind, gives an idea of the rotten condition implied. The combination of indifference and inertia brings one to the state of decay. One is faced with the situation where things are going to ruin, as if through poison or venomous worms complacently breeding in a bowl. One is reminded that those who follow another will have a price to pay, and here we have a clear indication of how troublesome the condition will be to correct. Hard work is indicated, but great progress can be made, and success will come to one who deals properly with the situation. Consider carefully all the events that have brought on the decay, and the measures that will be necessary to remedy it. Caution is advised after beginning any campaign, to avoid any potential relapse. The turning-point will eventually be reached, with disorder giving way to order. The decay has been brought about by inner weakness, and the superior person will nourish his own virtue when he helps others. Once the people have been stirred to remove the corruption, then they will be able to receive the benefits and blessings of the virtuous conditions that result. The end of confusion is the beginning of order.

The image is of the wind being driven back from the foot of a mountain, scattering things about in a disorderly way.

THE LINES

1 | Decay has developed from clinging to outdated habit. The situation is perilous, but can be corrected. There will be good fortune in the end.

2 | One must be gentle and firm in dealing with decay that is brought about by inner weakness. Find the middle way.

3 | Over-enthusiastic reform will meet with resistance. No harm is done, and one's good intentions are recognized.

4 | Make sure that all traces of past corruption have been eliminated before trying to move forward. There is no gain in tolerating decay.

5 | With able helpers, one will be able to instigate new reforms, creating goodwill among friends and colleagues.

6 | Do not become complacent. Withdraw from the situation if you have nothing more to contribute; but do not sit back and criticize.

APPROACH

APPROACH is the symbol of advance. The compliant earth positioned over the joyous water reflects the correct relationship that exists between people of different characters. The strong and highly placed descends freely, to bring the high and low closer together. The combination of joy and forbearance paves the way for great progress and success when one remains firmly correct. The implications are favorable, as the light-giving forces expand from within. The hexagram represents the twelfth month of the year, at a time just after the winter solstice, when the sun's light begins once again to ascend. Action undertaken at this time will be powerful and succeed, so long as it is governed by utmost honesty. Caution that is grounded on the changing character of all conditions and events will prevent one from making serious mistakes. The light-giving forces will, in time, recede, and the advancing power will decay. The threat of misfortune will be avoided when one meets the danger head on—before it has had a chance to become reality, and thus infect the social climate. The superior person will work inexhaustibly for the good of all mankind. His compassion is limitless. No part of humanity is excluded from his teaching.

The image is of the deep lake, whose moisture gives nourishment to the broad earth and all the creatures sustained on it.

THE LINES

1 | Advance in the company of others who are moving upward; but don't be carried away recklessly. Through firm correctness there will be good fortune.

2 | When one truly understands and acts in accordance with the laws of life, advancing with others of similar accord will be advantageous.

3 | Danger lies in becoming relaxed and over-confident when things go well. When one shows remorse for this mistaken attitude, there will be no error.

4 | One who openly draws another person of high ability to advance with him will bring favor to both.

5 | A wise ruler will attract people of ability, who will expertly manage their own affairs without his interference.

6 | The benefits of honest and generous conduct are success and harmony for all.

OBSERVATION

OBSERVATION is the symbol of both contemplation and manifestation; indicating the act of showing, or manifesting, as well as looking at, or contemplating. The trigram wind, with the attributes of flexibility and penetration, moves with vigor over that of the docile earth. The hexagram itself, with the two strong (yang) lines, positioned over the four weak (yin) ones, gives the physical appearance of a viewing tower. From this vantage point one is able to see for miles around, just as the tower itself is visible from a great distance. The wise ruler observes the laws of heaven, and manifests them in his good behavior. As the four seasons proceed without error in following the spirit-like way of heaven, so too are the people influenced by one who lives according to divine law. The hexagram Observation represents the eighth month, a time when people begin to gather in the harvest, but are not yet able to enjoy the bounty. In spiritual practice there is a similar moment, when the worshipper has already washed his hands but has not yet presented the offering. Contemplation of the sincerity and dignity of this most solemn moment of meditation transforms all who witness it. The influence of the superior person extends to all the people; just like the wind that moves over the whole earth.

The image is of the flexible wind, spreading itself over the whole surface of the docile earth.

THE LINES

1 | One who cannot see far, and therefore takes superficial views, will not be blamed. One who can see, but does not, will have cause for regret.

2 | A narrow view will result in narrow behavior; this is appropriate only for small tasks of an inward nature.

3 | Self-examination will give one the objectivity needed to determine whether the proper course of action is to advance or to recede.

4 | One who is stirred to ambition from a balanced view, rather than an egotistical one, will be rewarded.

5 | A person who occupies a position of authority over others must pay special attention to the effects of his actions. Self-contemplation is indicated.

6 | When one is finally liberated, contemplation of the self will give way to contemplation of the laws of life.

BITING THROUGH

BITING THROUGH is the symbol of criminal proceedings. The bright intelligence of the upper trigram, fire, unites with the majestic movement of the lower trigram, thunder, resulting in the brilliant manifestation of thunder and lightning. The fact that these two elements accompany each other in nature furthers the cause of union that is prevalent in the hexagram. Remove the obstacles to union, and high and low will come together with a proper understanding. The force of legal constraints is necessary, and when these are applied intelligently there will be success. The punishment must always be in proportion to the nature of the crime. As lightning yields to the roar of thunder, so let leniency temper the most severe judgements. The superior person will not hesitate to take vigorous measures against those who attempt to disrupt the harmony of social life, bearing in mind that unrestrained harshness will be no more effective that unrestrained gentleness toward the offender. Penalties imposed with intelligence are an effective means of publicizing the enforcement of just, well-founded laws. When it is one's responsibility to inflict the punishment, let all one's actions be governed by clarity and compassion.

The image is of the light-giving clarity of lightning, being joined by the strength of thunder to create respect among all creatures.

THE LINES

1 | Small punishments are in order for small offenses. Halt crime before it has a chance to progress.

2 | Severe punishment is required in proportion to the crime, and must be continued until the end is secured. Avoid over-reacting and there will be no error.

3 | Old problems must be confronted and firmly dealt with if one is to remain free from blame.

4 | One will need to be as hard as steel and as straight as an arrow to overcome the present obstacles. Recognize the difficulty of the situation, and remain firm.

5 | There is danger in being too lenient. Heed the warning, and find the middle way. Responsibilities increase.

6 | There will be evil if one remains deaf to counsel and persists in wrong actions.

GRACE

GRACE is the symbol of what is ornamental, and of the act of adornment. The arresting qualities of the trigram mountain, here in position over the burning force of fire, give way to the light that shines forth from deep inside the mountain. The fire sends up its light to illuminate and beautify all things. As there is ornament in nature, so should there be in society; but its place is secondary to what is substantial. The sun's light is accepted as the essential source that brings life to all living things; yet it is through the various movements and relative positions of the moon and stars that we come to distinguish between night and day. By contemplating the movements of heavenly forms, we begin to understand the changing demands of the universe. The social ceremonies and performances that regulate and beautify relationships among people are enhanced by elegance and adornment. But adornment, in order to be useful, must be restrained by substance. By contemplating the social forms, it becomes possible to further the progress of humanity. Graceful, ordered human behavior develops when the light of love is reflected in the firmness of justice. The attributes presented by the hexagram Grace, of clarity within and quiet without, indicate the advantageous position of quiet contemplation and rest. Bear in mind that all great matters of judgement demand the simple, unornamented truth.

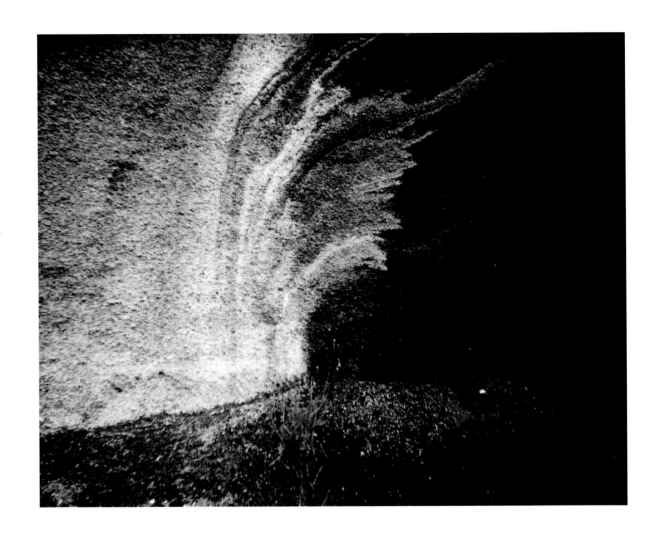

The image is of the light and clarity of fire, issuing forth from the arresting nature of the mountain, and showering its elegance on all.

THE LINES

1 | Abandon all superficial luxury and indulgence. Walk gracefully and with dignity, rather than ride in a carriage acquired by unscrupulous means.

2 | Let what is substantial command and rule what is merely ornamental, in much the same way as the chin is simply adorned by the beard.

3 | When one is fortunate enough to be blessed with rich favors, remain correct and firm to ensure their continuance.

4 | Beware the danger of exaggerated grace. The arousal of doubt indicates the superiority of solidarity and the transcendental power of love.

5 | When one's offerings are presented with sincerity, even though they may be small, good fortune will result.

6 | Ornament has run its course, and now there is a return to pure simplicity. At the height of development, all ornament is discarded.

SPLITTING APART

SPLITTING APART is the symbol of collapse and dispersion, as in falling or being overthrown. The trigram mountain rests on top of the docile earth, preventing any progress for the moment. The positions of the trigrams also reflect the way in which the mountain adheres to the earth, and so offers guidance for the wise ruler to seek to strengthen those below him, thus securing the peace and stability of his own position, which is now clearly being challenged from below. It is beneficial to note the application of the symbol of dispersion to the natural world, as well as that of the socio-political. The hexagram Splitting Apart represents the ninth month, when the beauty and glory of summer have disappeared, and the year is ready to fall into the sterile times of winter. Without this time of inner docility and devotion, coupled with outward stillness, we would not experience the workings of the laws of heaven, as they alternate between increase and decrease, emptiness and fullness. In political terms, small (weak) men have gradually displaced the strong ones, until only one remains—represented by the topmost line of the hexagram. The lesson for this person is to wait. The power operating against him at the moment is too strong; but the fashion of political life changes as swiftly as the seasons. If he waits, a change for the better will shortly appear.

The image is of a mountain resting on the docile earth, waiting for the right moment to bring forth its blessings.

THE LINES

1 | Inferior forces are at work to undermine what is superior and strong. Destruction is imminent. One is advised to wait for the tide to recede.

2 | Extreme caution is advised. The danger persists, as the power of the inferior grows. Unsupported, stubborn persistence will only hasten the downfall.

3 | One must isolate oneself from the companionship of inferior people. Strive to develop an inner relationship with a superior person.

4 | Misfortune can no longer be avoided—it must be endured.

5 | As the dark forces come closer to the source of light, the energy changes and all people voluntarily submit to the laws of heaven.

6 | Splitting Apart culminates in the growth of new fruit from the disintegration of the old.

HEXAGRAM **2 4** | FU 復

RETURNING

RETURNING is the symbol of reversal. The trigram earth rests over that of the powerful thunder, which is enclosed and silent beneath her. In the previous hexagram we saw inferior people prevailing over superior men, all that is good in nature and society yielding to what is bad. But change is the law of nature and society. When decay has reached its climax, recovery will begin to take place. Returning belongs to the eleventh month, and hails the celebration of the winter solstice, when the sun turns back in his course, and begins to move with a constant regular progress towards the summer solstice. These harmonious changes of nature are reflected in the political and social lives of men. The first tentative steps that the wanderer takes towards his return to virtue, or friends take towards understanding after estrangement, are mirrored in the first genial stirrings in the earth that follow the winter solstice. As the spring of life has to be nursed in quietness, so also is the purpose of good nourished by movement that develops within and manifests itself in devotion without. The arousing thunder is just beginning, and will be strengthened by its restful position under the earth. The movement of the heavenly revolution refers to the regular alternation of darkness and light, and cold and heat, that are prevalent in the different months of the year.

The mind of heaven and earth is visible in the love of life, and in all forms of goodness that a person experiences in the depths of his soul when he encounters his divine essence.

The image is one of returning energy. The thunder that is nourished under the docile nature of the earth is renewed.

THE LINES

1 | The act of returning implies that there has been some deviation. Immediate return brings great good fortune.

2 | Good fortune comes when one admirably sets aside one's pride and follows the advice of a wiser person.

3 | There is danger in continually having to reverse one's position in order to return to the good path. Recognize this danger and there will be no error.

4 | Even when walking with others, do not hesitate to change direction if necessary to follow your inner truth.

5 | If one's previous diversions have been extreme, be prepared to make a public apology. Such sincerity will give no cause for regret.

6 | If a person obstinately refuses the opportunity to return, he will bring long-lasting calamities on to himself.

FREEDOM FROM ERROR

FREEDOM FROM ERROR is the symbol of innocence. The subject of this hexagram is one who is entirely free from recklessness and insincerity. The trigram heaven positioned over that of thunder indicates great progress and success for one who is innocent and free from cunning and deceit. The motive power of thunder is reinforced by the strength of heaven, and it will not be advantageous for one to try to proceed, even though one has fallen into error. When misfortune comes to one who is innocent by nature, it will pass away without serious result. The quality of innocence is an expression of the highest laws of heaven, and therefore represents a highly developed state of humanity. Innocence is considered to be a noble attribute; and an absolute degree of honesty is essential to it. The closer a person comes to expressing the ideals of this quality in daily life, the more powerful will be his influence, and the greater his success. When the superior person is motivated by devotion to the divine spirit within, his actions will instinctively be correct. His innocence will lead him to do what is right, without any expectation of reward or personal advancement; much like the flowers that respond to the creative forces of spring. The good ruler will draw upon this source of spiritual wealth, to enhance the development of all who come under his influence.

The image is of thunder rolling under the whole sky, calling on all things to express their primal innocence.

THE LINES

1 | Good fortune results from actions undertaken with confidence, based on one's sincere inner truth.

2 | When all one's actions are entirely free from selfish motives, anything undertaken will meet with success.

3 | Innocence alone will not protect one from misfortune. Take adequate precautions.

4 | One must make every effort to remain firm and correct, despite the influence of others. Caution is advised.

5 | Misfortune that has come about through no fault of one's own need not be eradicated by external means. Let nature take its course.

6 | The time to act has passed. Be still, and do not attempt to initiate any fresh movement.

MAJOR RESTRAINT

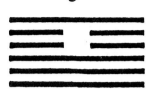

MAJOR RESTRAINT is the symbol of the great taming force, and of accumulation. The trigram mountain, representing substantial solidity, rests over the greatest strength of heaven. The increase of power, tamed by the force of keeping still, gives rise to the grand accumulation of virtue. Movement that is repressed and restrained accumulates its strength and thereby increases its power. The superior person will restrain strength within, by holding firmly to great creative sources. The conditions of Major Restraint apply to three different aspects of the idea of holding firm. They are: "holding together," as heaven within the mountain; "holding back," restraining the strong; and "holding," as in caring for or nourishing. One is reminded that people are held together by a strong, clear-headed ruler. One who is able to keep still will experience a daily renewal of energy that will sustain him at the height of his powers. The love and devotion that one gives to sacred doctrine will replenish his own strength of character. A wise man enriches himself when he studies the past. He does not simply acquire knowledge; he learns to apply it for the benefit of all mankind. When one rules in harmony with heaven, even difficult undertakings succeed.

The image is of the great power of heaven being restrained within the mountain, until the time is right for its release.

1 | Danger is at hand. It is advantageous to halt any plan of advance. Use the time constructively, and wait for a more harmonious opportunity.

2 | The energy that one accumulates through waiting with awareness will be needed for the difficult times ahead.

3 | When the obstacles are removed, one is advised to move forward with like-minded people. The threat of danger will be overcome by remaining firm and correct.

4 | Perilous conditions are circumvented when one takes measures of precaution.

5 | Look to the cause of the danger; not at its symptoms. Cutting the roots will bring cause for congratulations.

6 | The work of repression is over. Accumulated virtue is released with a powerful influence.

NOURISHMENT

NOURISHMENT is the symbol of sustenance, and is represented by the upper jaw. The solid trigram mountain positioned over that of moving thunder gives the image of tranquil movement. The two undivided lines at the top and bottom of the hexagram, with four undivided lines in between, suggest the appearance of an open mouth. The bottom line denotes upward movement, and forms the lower jaw, part of the mobile chin. The top line denotes that which is solid, or keeping still, and forms the more fixed upper jaw. The open lines in the middle signify the cavity of the mouth. One may be called on to nourish one's own body, mind or spirit, or that of someone else. Each person will have to determine the right course of action relevant to the particular set of circumstances. Where food and drink nourish the body, virtue is nourished by words. One must use discrimination in deciding whom or what to nourish, as well as in the sustenance that one seeks for oneself. A wise man moves his jaw with care. He does not risk injuring what is important for the sake of what is unimportant. He uses words carefully, in harmony with what is right, and he is moderate in all matters of food and drink. When the nourishment is correct, there will be good fortune.

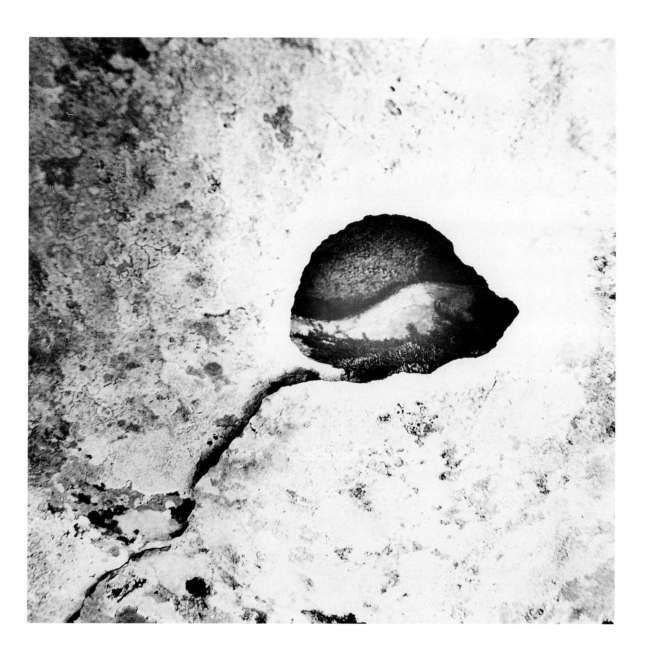

The image is one of tranquil motion. Thunder stirs within the calm of the mountain, signaling the rain that will nourish all things.

THE LINES

1 | Be aware of any feelings of envy that arise, and counter them by developing your own self worth.

2 | Do not shirk responsibilities. A person who deviates from his own true nature will find misfortune.

3 | Pleasures that merely satisfy the senses will not provide nourishment. Failure to recognize this brings cause for regret.

4 | One who is committed to working for the nourishment of all will need good helpers. Seek them diligently, and there will be no error.

5 | One may need to retire from action in order to receive guidance from a higher source. This is not the time to take on great projects.

6 | When one is in harmony with the source of all nourishment, even great and difficult tasks can be undertaken, and all will benefit.

LARGE EXCESS

LARGE EXCESS is the symbol of major preponderance. The arrangement of the trigram water over that of wind (or wood) indicates that there will be advantage in moving in the proper direction, and that there will be success. This hexagram is comprised of two weak lines positioned at the top and bottom, with four strong ones in between: exactly the opposite of what was presented in the previous hexagram, Nourishment. This gives the appearance of a great beam, weak at the ends, and therefore unable to sustain its own weight. The implication is of extraordinary times that will require extraordinary gifts in the conduct of affairs during them. Troubles are inevitable, but the strong lines show the ability of the subject to respond to them. The wise man will maintain flexibility and humbleness in everything that he does; his actions will be distinguished by their carefulness, and the solution will come through diligent assessment of the situation. The lower trigram, in its expression of wood, indicates trees under water—a flood. This is certainly an extraordinary time, and one is advised to follow the example of the tree that stands joyfully rooted in itself, even when covered by the temporary waters of the flood. The times are indeed dangerous, and must not continue. As the flood waters will eventually recede, so will whatever is in excess, whether

pleasant or sorrowful, give way to its opposite. Thus the superior man is able to stand up alone when necessary, without fear, and retire from the world without regret.

The image is of the waters of a lake, rising over the tops of the trees that have been submerged when the weak boundaries of the banks collapsed.

THE LINES

1 | Great caution is advised. Pay careful attention to what may seem to be insignificant tasks when laying the foundation for any undertaking.

2 | Partnerships and alliances formed from previously neglected sources of nourishment will bring rejuvenation and advancement.

3 | Obstinate or stubborn behavior will alienate one from the only possible source of support.

4 | The good fortune that results from the support that one gains through friendship is contingent on the fact that one's trust is never abused.

5 | In extremely difficult times, one must take particular care to maintain fairness and balance in all relationships.

6 | So long as a person's intentions are to satisfy the good of mankind, even if his actions fail, he will suffer no blame.

ABYSMAL

ABYSMAL is the symbol of sinking. The doubling of the trigram water indicates a perilous cavity or pit. Danger is apparent in the depths of a ravine with water flowing through it. The movement of the water is constant, and eventually it flows over its confines. The superior person maintains the virtue of his heart and the integrity of his conduct constantly and in all matters. He practices the business of instructing others with the utmost honesty and sincerity. The hexagram Abysmal represents one whose mind is sharpened and whose spirit is strengthened by the contact with danger. Water shows the right direction to take when a dangerous situation presents itself. Its natural inclination is to sink. It fills up all deep places, and will only rise to the top of its container while seeking to flow downward again. Nothing can make water shed its essential nature; it remains true to itself under all conditions. Thus will the sincere man be able to penetrate the meaning of every situation by remaining true to his inner self. The Abysmal represents the deepest core of man, his soul that is confined by the body. So too, will it rise to the top and overflow when the time is right. One is advised to follow the example of water in all one's teachings, and be forever consistent and dependable. By fostering the good in one's own nature, one will avoid disaster.

The image is of water flowing in a deep ravine, penetrating all places, and moving in a constant direction.

THE LINES

1 | When a person grows accustomed to danger, he runs the risk of becoming indifferent to it, and thus all his efforts will only involve him more deeply in the danger.

2 | If unable to escape altogether from the danger, do not become more deeply involved in it. Remain calm, and endure the difficult situation.

3 | Take no action at this time. Any movement, forward or backward, up or down, will only increase the danger. One must wait for the clear way out to be revealed.

4 | In dangerous times, let sincerity replace all rigorous customs and rituals. Simplify everything, and there will be no cause for error.

5 | Do not attempt to push the situation too far. Be like water, and pursue the path of least resistance.

6 | When one has lost the way of heaven, there is no escape from danger. The consequences will be long-lasting, though not permanent.

CLINGING

CLINGING is the symbol of adherence. Doubling the trigram fire indicates fire and light. Its virtue is brightness, which reflects the attribute of clarity. Fire has no definitive form of its own, but clings to the burning object, and thus is bright. The fire and light generated by the sun also represent a natural metaphor for intelligence. The double brightness indicated by the hexagram Clinging will require a strict adherence to what is correct, as well as a docile humbleness. The outgoing energy symbolized by fire is constantly being used up. Therefore it must have some enduring inner source that perseveres, otherwise it would burn itself out. All that gives light is dependent on something to which it clings. As the sun and moon cling to heaven, the superior person clings to what is right. By cultivating an attitude of compliance and voluntary dependence on the laws of heaven, one will develop clarity that is free from arrogance. Motivating energy, like fire, must be controlled for it to be constructive and to avoid becoming destructive. One is advised to follow this example, and curb excessive behavior and attitudes. The superior person will carefully cultivate his brilliant virtue, and spread its brightness over all the land. By the clarity of his nature, his influence will reach far and wide, and penetrate ever more deeply into the nature of man. Fire that clings to a source of inner clarity produces a light that endures.

The image is of the light of the sun that spreads its radiance over the whole earth.

THE LINES

1 | Danger lies in moving forward too quickly and without composure or clarity. Serious concentration is needed.

2 | Relationships formed on mutual trust and respect will bring good fortune. Harmony results from following the middle way.

3 | As the sun rose, so will it also set. A calm acceptance of natural law will help one to avoid foolish excesses.

4 | Conserve your energy. Remember that wood is consumed by the fire that clings to it. Do not become over-excited and lose your inner clarity.

5 | A genuine change of heart is needed for one to develop a peaceful and virtuous nature. Tears may flow, but good fortune is indicated.

6 | The change is complete. Show generous consideration to all people who have been affected. Make the transition as smooth as possible.

INFLUENCE

INFLUENCE, or wooing, is the symbol of mutual influence. The trigram water, being the weaker, positioned over the strength of the mountain, indicates influences moving and responding to each other in a positive way. When the strong willingly subordinates itself to the needs of the weak, the two unite. The result will be a mutually caring union, the success of which is determined by the effects of mutual attraction. The interaction of the trigrams, in both influencing and being influenced by each other, conveys the notion of a free and successful course of action. As with people, it is through their natural affinity for each other that this exchange takes place. For influence to be effective it must be correct in itself, and correct in its end. It will be free from all selfish gains, and motivated purely from the heart. Such influence will be effective and fortunate. The quiet persistence of the mountain finds a joyful companion in the lake, thus furthering the idea of stimulation. A harmonious, successful relationship develops when one's joy is prevented from going to extremes by keeping still within. The laws of nature are reflected in the great benefits that occur from the mutual attraction of apparently opposite forces. It is through their attraction for one another that heaven and earth exert their influences and ensure the transformation and

production of all things. In this way, the superior person influences the minds of others, with great humbleness and an empty self.

The image is of the waters from a lake or marsh, placed high above the lands, that will descend to bring nourishment to all below.

THE LINES

1 | The desire to influence is not enough. Although the intention may be good, actions undertaken out of anxiety will have no benefit.

2 | Wait patiently for the source of real influence to present itself. Abide quietly, without worry, and there will be success.

3 | Resist the impulse to foolishly follow everything that moves. Be cautious. Impulsive actions bring cause for regret.

4 | When one's actions are firm and correct, their influence will reach far and wide. When they are wavering and uncertain, or in any way manipulative, few will follow.

5 | When one's actions are led by the heart, and totally devoid of selfish motivation; then one is free to influence and/or be influenced by others.

6 | One must never seek to influence others through flattery and idle talk.

DURATION

DURATION is the symbol of perseverance. The positioning of the trigram thunder over that of wind exhibits the natural state of the active leading the receptive. Thunder and wind possess the qualities of motivating force and docility. Their strength and weakness respond to each other. They are in mutual communication, and therefore they create an enduring and consistent relationship. The long continuance implicit in the hexagram Duration is based on the union of inner gentleness and outward movement. The idea of perseverance is applied to one who continually acts out the law of his being. Whatever a person's calling in life, he must remain firm and constant without becoming rigid or immobile. He must be able to adapt himself to changing circumstances by altering his outward behavior, but never his inner truth. The immutable laws that govern the cycles of heaven and earth determine that everything begins anew as it ends. It is only through following its complete course of waxing and waning that the light of the moon continues to shine. When two companions join forces as naturally as thunder and wind, both must be continually observant of what is correct in their own nature. The weak maintains flexibility in its submission, and the strong remains firm in its movement. Such actions will bring good fortune, and move successfully in any

direction. Contemplation of the enduring forces of nature will help one to remember that when the moving power is spent, it will begin again.

The image is of thunder rolling along with its natural companion wind, remaining firm in its mobility.

THE LINES

1 | The desire for long continuance at the beginning of any undertaking will be a hindrance. Only through careful and sensitive efforts can one achieve enduring results.

2 | Excessive enthusiasm and unrealistic goals must be abandoned. Then one is able to achieve a stable position and avoid difficulties.

3 | A person must continually maintain his inner certainty, and not give way to his easily excited superficial nature.

4 | When one deviates from one's inner certainty, all efforts will be in vain. One must seek in the right way if anything is to be found.

5 | Be consistent. By remaining true to one's nature one will pursue what is right in each particular situation.

6 | Enduring relationships cannot be forced. One is advised to discontinue all frantic activity and regain one's inner composure. Thus will violent efforts be avoided.

RETREAT

RETREAT is the symbol of regression or withdrawal. The trigram heaven positioned over that of the mountain indicates the correct way for one to withdraw from lesser forces. The superior person, in accordance with this, keeps inferior people at a distance, not by showing that he hates them, but by his own dignified reserve. The encroachment of "inferior" people is related to the sixth month, when the forces of winter are already beginning to be felt. It is the same condition under which the power of light retreats to security when the power of the dark begins to ascend. Without this movement it would be impossible to distinguish night from day. Retreat does not mean running away. The emphasis is on dignified withdrawal, in accordance with the circumstances of the times. One is acutely aware of the potentially harmful results of remaining in the situation from which one must retreat. Withdrawal is imperative so as not to exhaust oneself unnecessarily. Strength will be found in paying attention to small matters, and waiting for the right moment, to ensure that the retreat does not become a desperate struggle. One is not abandoning anything or anyone; nor is there any semblance of hate or anger in one's retreat, for this would only create a subjective involvement which would bind one to the hated object. One is simply moving

away, in a dignified manner, and putting as much distance as possible between oneself and the encroaching offenders. Constructive retreat is a means by which a person may make successful progress on his life path, even in his retiring.

The image is one of a mountain rising further and further into the sky, as the sky continues to retreat before it.

THE LINES

1 | Do not hurry. The retreat is already under way, and one is dangerously exposed to negative influences. Hasty actions will only aggravate the danger.

2 | By remaining correct and firm in one's retreat, one will be able to hold fast to one's ideas and principles.

3 | Do not become entangled with people who will impede your movements. Keep your distance, and do not become too familiar with any of them.

4 | Once the decision has been taken to retreat, exercise it with determination. One who acts when full of regrets will not find success.

5 | When one retreats at the right time and in an admirable way, one will attract others of a similar outlook and avoid severing existing links completely.

6 | A vigorously and happily executed retreat will be advantageous in every respect.

GREAT STRENGTH

GREAT STRENGTH is the symbol of major power. The trigram thunder positioned over that of heaven indicates an abundance of strength and vigor. It implies a time when the great are becoming strong. When strength is held in subordination to the idea of what is right, and exerted only in harmony with it, then will it truly become a major power. It is the union of strength within and movement without that forms the very basis of this power. Perseverance is essential if one is to avoid the danger of becoming too intent on movement, and therefore advancing before the time is right. True greatness depends on constant harmony with what is right, and the wise man will not take a step that is not in accordance with this harmony. Great Strength denotes a power that has already passed the mid-point, hence there is the possibility that one may mistakenly attribute this power to oneself and forget to inquire continually into what is right. One must take care to avoid the great dangers of excess and misuse of power. Authentic power does not degenerate into mere force, but remains inwardly united with the fundamental principles of what is right and just. The power of man becomes a reflection of the great power that we see working in nature, when it is exercised impartially and unselfishly.

The image is of thunder, rolling across the sky and making all things shake, thus giving expression to the great power within.

THE LINES

1 | Advancing by force will only lead to exhaustion. Resist impulsive and reckless behavior.

2 | With firm correctness there will be good fortune. Take a pause from all activity. Act properly and develop an inner calm.

3 | The situation is dangerous. One must take care to avoid the misuse of power, and to avoid injury by not exerting all one's strength.

4 | Going forward cautiously will produce good results. Obstacles disappear, and, with them, any cause for repentance.

5 | Strength must be controlled and directed in order to be effective. Discard any stubborn or aggressive behavior.

6 | Arrogance and stubbornness can only lead to deadlock. Accept the situation, and take the time to rest and reflect.

ADVANCE

ADVANCE is the symbol of progress. The trigram fire positioned over that of earth gives clear indication of the powerful light of the sun shining more and more to perfect the day. The superior person, in accordance with this, gives himself totally to the task of allowing his own bright virtue to shine even more brilliantly. In Advance we see the clarity of fire spreading itself without restraint over the totally receptive earth. The indication is of the sun rising above the earth, which may be full of dark clouds, and then traveling on to its meridian height. At this point the power of the sun dispels the force of the dark, and the shadows are removed. The true nature of man is reflected in this natural progress: he is born pure, but becomes clouded by his involvement in circumstances that have themselves become cloudy. Through purification he is able to restore his own inner clarity and, following the example of the sun, shine his light on all living beings. The docile submissiveness of the earth, as she receives the nurturing rays of the sun, reflects the peace and tranquility that people experience when in the presence of one who truly manifests his inner light.

The image is of the sun fully risen over the face of the earth, before it begins its cyclical descent.

1 | Meet any resistance or obstruction to progress with a large and generous mind, and there will be no error. Trust must be earned.

2 | Great blessings will come from one who is himself free from error. The sadness will pass, and harmony result.

3 | In an atmosphere of mutual trust and respect, like-minded people will progress naturally.

4 | If one sneaks around like a rat, rather than exposing oneself to the light of truth, there will be cause for regret.

5 | Remain reserved. The progress referred to is not about material success or failure, but about inner development.

6 | Let compassion guide the administration of any necessary form of punishment. Act with firm correctness.

DARKENING OF THE LIGHT

DARKENING OF THE LIGHT is the symbol of lack of appreciation. The trigrams earth and fire are now reversed from their positions in the preceding hexagram, Advance, and we have the indication of repressed or wounded intelligence. The light of the sun appears to be sinking into the earth, and therefore the effects of its brightness are obscured. In times of darkness, it will be advantageous to realize the severity of the difficulties in the situation, and maintain firm correctness. The superior person will recognize the futility of attempting to shine light where darkness prevails, and will therefore withdraw completely from the situation if necessary. One must remain grounded in one's own inner light, so as not to be swept away by the dark, unconscious circumstances that are in effect. It will be beneficial to maintain a pliant, yielding outer nature, like the earth, to protect and nourish the flame of inner consciousness. Under such conditions, one shows one's intelligence by keeping it obscured from negative forces. Be careful not to make any outward show of hostility, or unwittingly fall into the trap of trying to fight fire with fire. Let all actions be tempered with respect and consideration, even in the face of great difficulties. Perseverance will be rewarded.

The image is of the afterglow of the setting sun. The fire itself may appear to have sunk into the earth; but the light is veiled, not extinguished.

THE LINES

1 | A setback at the beginning of an undertaking offers an excellent opportunity to withdraw from the struggle and re-evaluate the situation.

2 | Good fortune will come to one who has the sensibility to recognize that others are also in danger, and offers help.

3 | Even when one encounters the source of negative influences directly, one must not be overly eager to try to change everything at once.

4 | One understands the full power of the darkening forces, and successfully escapes with little damage.

5 | If one is unable to withdraw completely from the situation, one should take great care to remain correct and firm in all actions.

6 | A person who has the opportunity to enlighten others, and chooses instead to injure them, will suffer his own obscurity in the end.

FAMILY

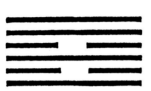

FAMILY is the symbol for the members of a household or clan. The trigram wind positioned over that of fire becomes representative of the family circle and the wide world outside it. The relationships that exist between various members of the family are merely reflections of the relations and positions that one finds in all social organizations everywhere. The symbolic positioning of wind over fire also indicates the power that the spoken word carries when it is delivered from the heart. The superior person is aware of this, and orders his words according to the truth of things. He is also careful to make sure that his conduct reflects the content of his words with uniform consistency. The subject of the hexagram is the regulation of the social unit, which is most effectively maintained through the joyful co-operation of the two forces at work—the clarity of fire and the gentleness of wind. These qualities translate into the strong authority that is needed to guide the family, coupled with the gentle loyalty and perseverance that are strengthened by the wind. When each member conducts himself with firm correctness, in relation to his particular situation within the group, then the results will be rewarding.

The image is of the light of fire being enhanced and carried forth by the wind.

THE LINES

1 | Regulations must be clearly defined at the beginning of a project. Then even their strict observance will not be felt as an imposition.

2 | Every member has a vital role to fulfill in the organization. Be careful not to make prejudiced judgements about their worth.

3 | Stern severity may be needed to silence a chattering mind, and thus avoid the consequences of untempered laxity and indulgence.

4 | The integrity of the unit will be maintained when there are genuine affection and harmony among the members.

5 | Mutual love grows naturally in an environment that is founded on trust and respect.

6 | When a person accepts the position of leader, he must take full responsibility for the influence of his actions on those following him.

DIVISION

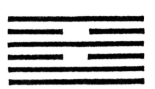

DIVISION is the symbol of opposition. The positioning of the trigram fire, whose natural tendency is to move upwards, over that of water, whose inclination is downwards, gives the impression of two forces which are moving away from each other. This interpretation reflects a social state in which division and mutual alienation prevail. A closer look at the trigrams reveal the expressions of the bright intelligence of fire, coupled with the harmonious satisfaction of water, to represent different—perhaps even opposite—objectives. These opposite forces, when allowed to act without malice or animosity towards each other, take on a totally different characteristic. One is reminded of how diametrically opposite are the natures of heaven and earth. They are, without a doubt, separate and apart from each other, yet the work that they do is related. The very fact that male and female are separate and apart is celebrated when their energies combine to create new life. It is as a result of their condition of disunity and separation that something totally new and unique can be born. The superior person, recognizing this, will be able to accept that there is diversity, even in matters that require general agreement. The natures of fire and water are different; but their very opposition creates the need for a bridge, thus paving the way for reconciliation.

The image is of fire blazing above the lake, the flames climbing towards heaven, the water flowing downward.

1 | Whatever has been lost will return by itself when the time is right. Open communication will help to silence slanderous tongues.

2 | Separation and disunity mark the times. A chance meeting will prove useful, and may lead to better understanding.

3 | What appears in the beginning to be only disorder and disunity will, in the long run, give way to order and union.

4 | One is isolated amidst the prevailing disunion. It is time to join together with like-minded people.

5 | Going forward with people with whom one feels a natural affinity will give cause for congratulations.

6 | When one feels isolated, it is easy to mistrust even the right people. Good fortune will greet the passing away of all doubts.

OBSTRUCTION

OBSTRUCTION is the symbol of difficulty. The trigram water, this time in the form of a cloud positioned over that of a steep and difficult mountain, indicates that there is danger both above and below. The superior person, in accordance with this, will take the opportunity to turn inward and examine himself and cultivate his virtue. The only way that the difficulty can possibly be overcome will be through the exercise of prudent caution. When one encounters danger without, one must be able to keep still within. The obstruction is not seen as a permanent condition. Rather, it is more of a character builder and, if approached sensibly, can offer a great occasion for self-development. The danger implied is in relation to movement, the timing of which is critical to coping successfully with the difficult situation. The arduous task of governing any sort of social organization will require the delicate balance of correct and firm activity, tempered by discreet inactivity when appropriate. One is advised to make a careful calculation of the circumstances, and take advantage of those that promise success in an enterprise; but have the courage to shun those that threaten difficulty and failure.

The image is of the clouds gathered over a steep and difficult mountain, providing one with the atmosphere to turn inwards for reflection.

THE LINES

1 | If one attempts to advance too soon, one will be overwhelmed by the difficulties of the situation. Wait for a more favorable time.

2 | The difficulties are indeed great, but no blame will be attached to one whose actions are not motivated by a view to his own advantage.

3 | To advance unsupported is to court disaster. Wait for a better time, and cherish those people who do give their support.

4 | There is little that a person can do alone. He must cultivate the loyal attachments that have already been formed, and wait for the time when he will be required to act.

5 | When one has no choice but to confront the greatest of difficulties, like-minded friends will come to help.

6 | Avoid the temptation to withdraw too far from the situation. Seek guidance from the great spirit.

LOOSENING

LOOSENING is the symbol of deliverance. The positioning of the trigram thunder, which indicates movement, over that of the abysmal water, signifies that there will be escape from peril through movement. The symbolism is likened to the act of untying a knot in a skein of thread, or unraveling a complication of any kind. Loosening denotes a condition in which the obstructions and difficulties indicated by the preceding hexagram, Obstruction, have been removed. When no further active operations are necessary to secure the peace, it is wise to allow things to return to their normal conditions as soon as possible. If further operations are necessary, let them be carried through without delay. One should not be anxious to change all the old manners and customs. There will be good fortune in coming back to the old traditions, without trying to impose anything new. Just as the atmosphere is cleared by a good thunderstorm, the feeling of oppression is relieved in deliverance. Loosening is also the symbol of spring, the time when the buds of the plants and trees that produce the various fruits begin to burst forth. They are aided in their blossoming by the cleansing power of the rain. Likewise, the superior person will forgive the errors of those who previously presented the opposition, and deal gently with their transgressions.

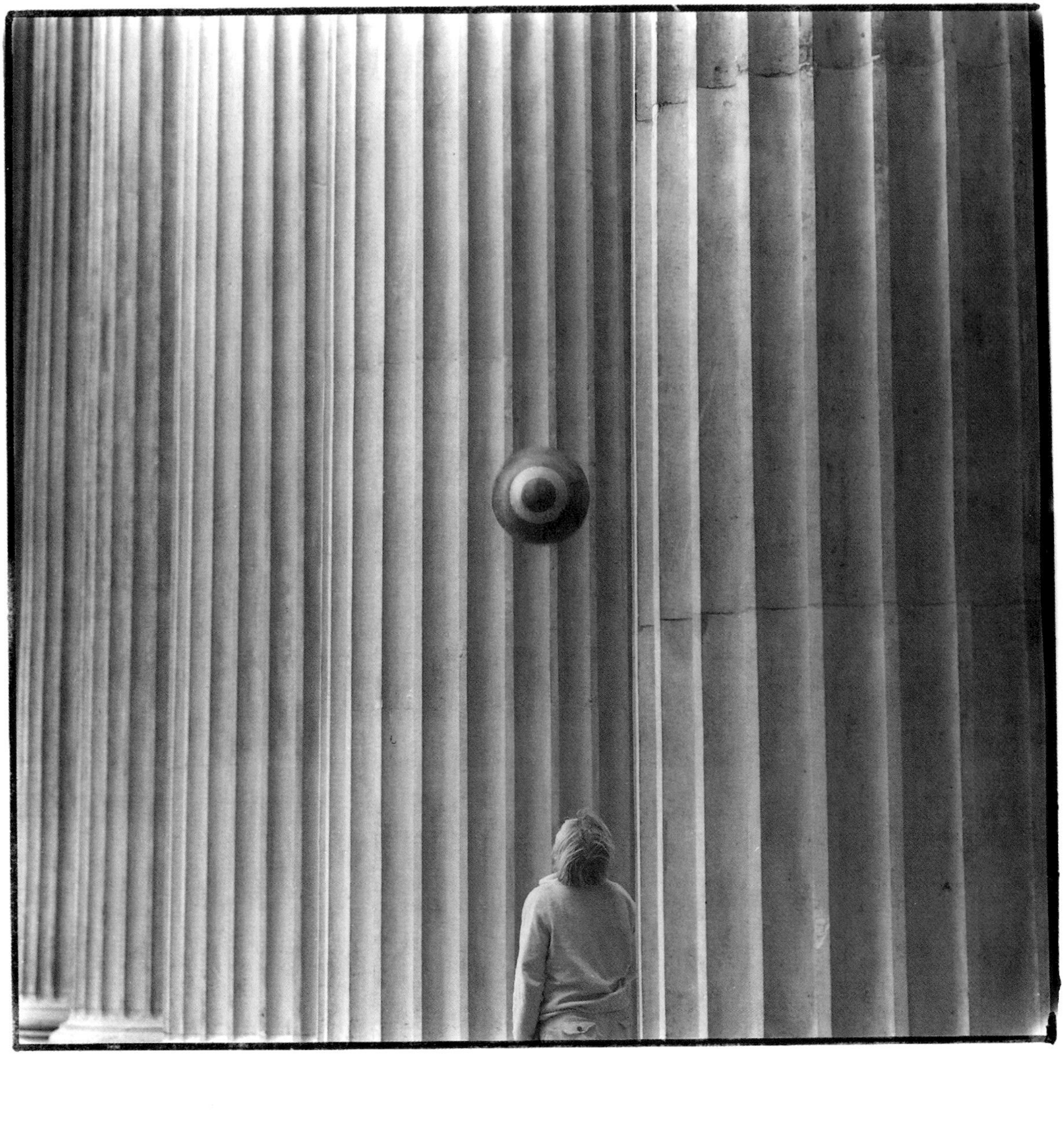

The image is of rolling thunder, with rain following that washes everything clean, in the early days of spring.

THE LINES

1 | One has survived the difficult times, and remains free from error. Rest quietly and enjoy the peace.

2 | Through firm, straightforward correctness one will remove cunning influences. To attempt to do so by brute force will only provoke indignation and rebellion.

3 | One must be careful and correct, particularly in times of affluence. Do not invite attack.

4 | Unions with untrustworthy people must be severed if one wants to establish relationships with trustworthy ones.

5 | Remove everything that is contrary to the establishment of peace and good order. Even inferior people will benefit from such earnest actions.

6 | Carefully directed, forceful methods must be enacted quickly. Only a person of utmost clarity should execute them, and only as a last resort.

DECREASE

DECREASE is the symbol of lessening or diminishing. The position of the trigram mountain over that of the lake allows it to receive the benefits of the rising (and therefore diminishing) vapors of the lake. All things on the mountain will grow greener because of the moisture that rises from the lake to sustain them. The mountain, as it symbolizes stubbornness or hardness, runs the risk of having this hardness turn into anger. The joyful attributes of the lake, if allowed to develop into hysterical gaiety and silliness, will simply expend themselves in wasted energy. The superior person, in accordance with this, will restrain his wrath and control his desires. Every diminution of what is in excess will bring it into accord with what is right and just. Let there be sincerity in this method of diminishing, and there will be great good fortune and the happiest results. The regulation of expenditure or contribution will vary according to the poverty or wealth of the individual. The social organizations will give according to the abundance or scantiness of their resources. Even if the contribution appear to be very small, it will be graciously accepted when it is offered with sincerity. There is a time when the strong should be diminished and the weak strengthened. Decrease and increase, overflow and emptiness, all take place in harmony with the conditions of the time.

The image is of the lake resting at the foot of the mountain, enriching all through its moisture.

THE LINES

1 | One can only give the other what he is able to receive. Give due consideration to your own needs.

2 | One is able to give help to the other without losing his own self-respect. Maintain firm correctness, and all will be well.

3 | One is more likely to find a significant relationship with another person when one travels alone, rather than with others.

4 | Willing helpers will appear when one is obviously making every effort to help oneself.

5 | This is a time of natural good luck. Accept it graciously.

6 | One who gives increase to others without diminishing one's own resources will attract the support of many able-bodied helpers.

INCREASE

INCREASE is the symbol of addition or increasing. The trigrams wind and thunder have the natural tendency to fortify each other, therefore their combination gives the idea of increase. When the docility of the wind is stimulated by the moving power of thunder, we experience daily advancement to an unlimited extent. There will be advantage in every movement undertaken at this time, as the increase is not restricted by place. In social organizations the hexagram Increase indicates a situation where the governing members are operating in order to dispense benefits to, and increase the resources of, all the people. What descends from above reaches to all below. The satisfaction of the people in such circumstances is without limit. The person who keeps this principle of increase in mind will be successful in all his enterprises and will overcome even the greatest of difficulties. Everything in this method of increase is regulated by the same requirements of time that cause the moon to wax and wane. Increase, by its very nature, is related to decrease. The superior person, when he sees what is good in others, moves towards it; when he sees the errors in his own ways, he turns away from those ways.

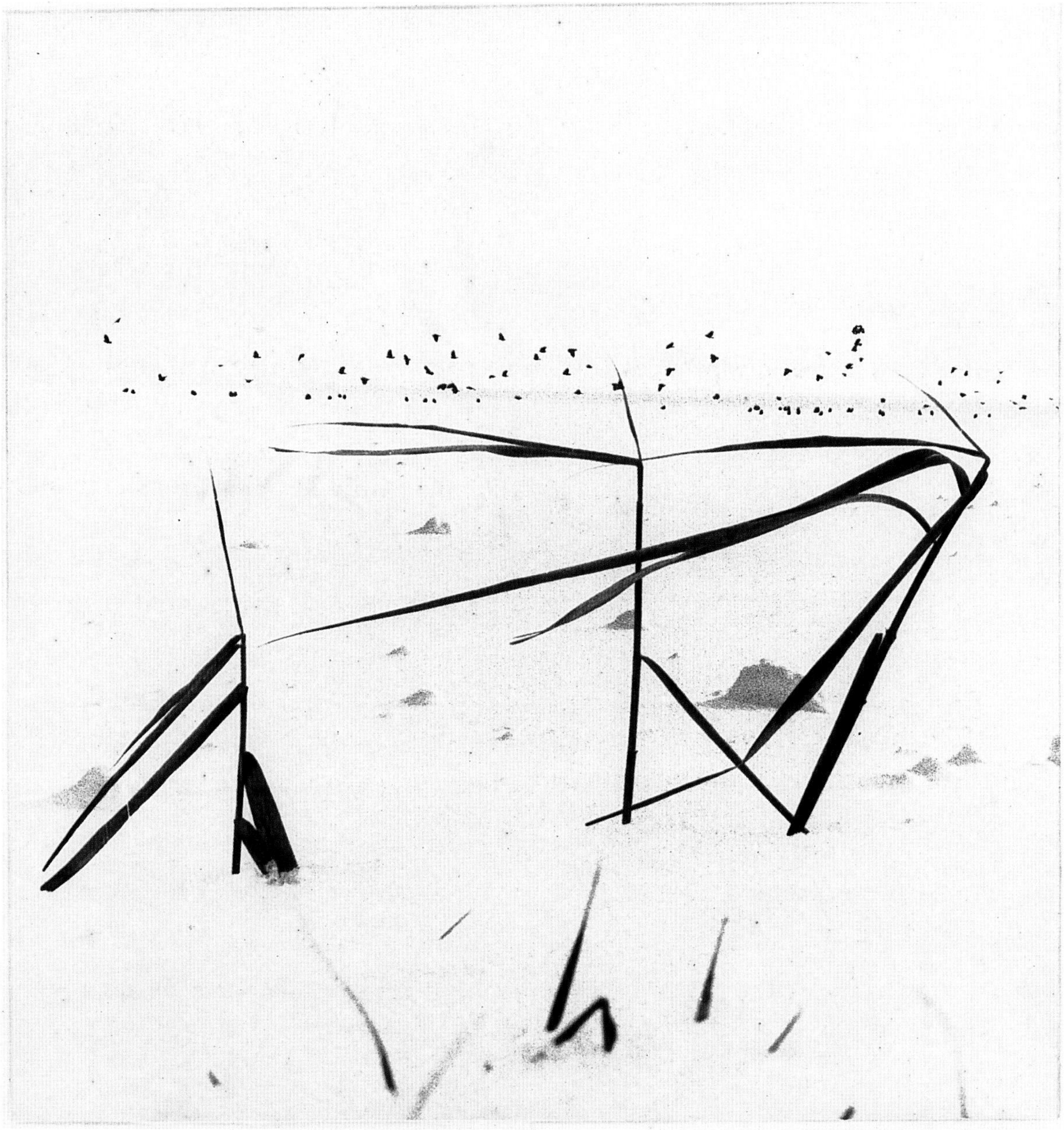

The image is of the forces of wind and thunder reinforcing and increasing each other.

THE LINES

1 | This is the time to make a great movement, the rashness of which will be forgiven. Guard against all forms of selfishness.

2 | Heaven confers benefits from above. Fortune is on one's side. Success is the result of remaining firm and correct.

3 | If one is sincere and pursues the middle way, even apparent misfortune will turn into advantage.

4 | When a person follows the middle path, rulers will listen to him and all below will benefit.

5 | The actions of a sincere heart are recognized by all. Great good fortune is indicated.

6 | Misfortune will come to one who strives only to benefit himself, without due regard for others. Heed the warning, and make any necessary changes now.

BREAK-THROUGH

BREAK-THROUGH is the symbol of resoluteness. With the trigram water positioned over that of heaven, we are introduced to the idea of a powerful cloudburst. The waters from the joyous lake have ascended into heaven in the form of vapors, and now they will shower again on to the earth. The break-through referred to by this hexagram comes as a welcome relief after a long accumulation of tension. It is seen as representing the third month of the year, when the last cold, dark remnants of winter will disappear before the advance of the warm, bright days of summer. In socio-political organizations, Breakthrough draws attention to the corrupt and powerful forces that have been in existence for too long, and are now ready to be abolished; just as naturally as the moon wanes after it is full. The superior person who finds himself involved in the removal of such practices will do so by following the guidance of his inner voice, and not by succumbing to hostile aggression. In this way he will secure the genuine support of all those who are affected by the situation. The cloudburst may take the form of openly denouncing the unacceptable practices, and one is advised to remain constantly aware of the difficulty and danger of the condition. Success will come to a person who makes it perfectly clear how unwillingly he has taken such strong action, and shares the benefits with everyone.

The image is of the joyous waters of a lake rising upward, and descending from heaven in a cloudburst.

THE LINES

1 | Do not attempt to move forward too soon, or without proper preparation. Find the strength to wait.

2 | Determination, tempered by caution, is needed to remove harmful influences within oneself, as well as from the environment.

3 | Be prepared to stand alone, even amidst gossip from others. Make every effort to communicate clearly.

4 | One who is obstinate will receive no benefit, even from sensible advice. Act sensitively towards everyone.

5 | One's close proximity to the source of negativity makes it even more difficult to eradicate it. Harmony will be found in the middle way.

6 | Do not become complacent. A person must be willing to examine his own faults honestly, and strengthen his relationships with like-minded people.

MEETING

▬▬▬▬▬▬▬▬▬▬
▬▬▬▬▬▬▬▬▬▬
▬▬▬▬▬▬▬▬▬▬
▬▬▬▬▬▬▬▬▬▬
▬▬▬▬▬▬▬▬▬▬
▬▬▬▬ ▬▬▬▬

MEETING is the symbol of coming to meet. The trigram heaven positioned over that of wind shows the wind blowing everything under the sky, penetrating everywhere, and producing its natural effects. The hexagram Meeting denotes the fifth month, when the first burst of spring has abated and been followed by full growth, which now gives way to the latter days of summer when the light and heat begin to decline. This decline, if allowed to increase without limitation, would eventually result in the death of the universe. Likewise in socio-political situations, when an unworthy person begins to put himself forward into a position of power, especially through cunning and manipulative ways, his influence must be checked. Otherwise, this negative force would go on growing, as he displaces one good person after another and fills the vacant seats with inferior people like himself. The superior person, in this instance, must enjoin the help of others to ensure that the natural cycles of increase and decrease are kept in balance. The meetings generated by the flexibility of wind are significantly unexpected, and may take place under unusual conditions. Meetings or encounters that happen spontaneously, yet honestly, offer the opportunity for seemingly opposing forces to meet each other without regret.

The image is of the wind blowing everything under heaven, and penetrating everywhere.

THE LINES

1 | Both internal and external restraints will be needed to repel the influence of one who abuses his position of power.

2 | One must do all that one can to prevent others from coming under the influence of negative forces.

3 | The situation is dangerous. One is tempted to join forces with the unworthy element. Great clarity is needed.

4 | One must be careful not to alienate oneself from others, out of one's own personal ambition.

5 | One is advised to keep wise plans carefully concealed until the time is ripe to unfold them. Virtuous behavior will be rewarded.

6 | If the situation becomes unbearable, one must not hesitate to withdraw completely from it. Do so gracefully, and remain composed.

GATHERING TOGETHER

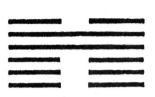

GATHERING TOGETHER is the symbol of collection. The trigram water, representing pleased satisfaction, positioned over that of the earth, representing devotion, indicates the condition of union or of being collected. The implication is that it is a happy union that prevails, when things are done in accordance with what is natural and practical for the conditions and requirements of the times. The waters of the lake are held together and in place by their banks, which preserve them from being indiscriminately dispersed. Sometimes dams and dykes are created to enhance the flow of the water, not to make it stagnant. Likewise, when people gather together of their own accord, the union that is formed must be preserved against those elements that could disturb and destroy it. One who accepts a position of leadership in such an organization must be prepared to resist attacks that arise from without, and to put down any sedition that may arise from within. The superior person will seek guidance in the spirit of his ancestors, and will call upon their wisdom to show him the way that is correct for the benefit of all members of the group. Spiritual ceremonies will be distinguished by their dignity and splendor, and all other activities will be conducted in harmony with them.

4

The image is of a lake, whose waters are gathered bountifully in the embrace of the earth.

THE LINES

1 | One is possessed with a desire for unity, but is unable to carry it out alone. Seek help from like-minded people, and tears will give place to smiles.

2 | One is encouraged and helped by the inner forces that bring people together. When offered with sincerity, even small contributions are acceptable.

3 | One may feel isolated from a group that has already been formed. Be courageous, and humbly seek an ally.

4 | When one works unselfishly for general unity, the rewards will be greatly fortunate. Be aware of the dangers of incorrect conduct.

5 | Confront immediately any mistrust or doubts that arise. Confidence will be earned, and all occasion for repentance will disappear.

6 | Tears of remorse, when one is unable to bring about the desired union, may open the door for reconciliation.

RISING AND ADVANCING

RISING AND ADVANCING is the symbol of pushing upward. The trigram earth, positioned over that of wood (also referred to as the gentle wind), indicates a time of advancing in an upward direction. The idea is expressed in the roots of a tree, planted beneath the obedient earth. The flexibility of the sapling is reflected in its gradual growth, which in turn symbolizes the upward advance of the superior person. Both of these processes are encouraged by the auspicious conditions of the time. A person will suddenly find himself advancing and ascending, not only because he has the qualities that enable him to carry out the advance, but also because he is presented with favorable opportunities to do so. The result of his advance will be fortunate, so long as he remains modest and adaptable to the situation. This is a vertical advance, from obscurity and lowliness to power and influence. One must carefully balance the applications of willpower and control to ensure that all movements are harmoniously conducted. To advance to the "south" implies movement to the regions of brightness and warmth, indicating that this will be a joyful progress. Pushing upward will involve an expenditure of energy, but one must be careful not to resort to violence. Remain gentle and devoted, as the wood that bends around objects as it grows upwards.

The image is of wood, rising and advancing through the earth to reach the sky.

THE LINES

1 | A person is encouraged in his advancement by like-minded others, which greatly increases his confidence in himself.

2 | Sincere and devoted loyalty will compensate for what may appear to be meager contributions.

3 | When a person has no doubt or hesitation, he runs the risk of behaving too boldly, and thus achieving nothing of lasting value.

4 | One is offered the opportunity to participate in great spiritual practices. There will be good fortune, and no mistakes will be made.

5 | One has advanced to the highest point of dignity through firm correctness. Great perseverance will be needed to remain there.

6 | When a person has reached the greatest height he is advised to think of retiring. Otherwise, blind ambition will bring cause for regret.

OPPRESSION

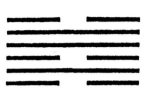

OPPRESSION is the symbol of repression. The positioning of the trigram water, as represented by a satisfied lake, over that of the perilous waters of a ravine, certainly suggest a condition of distress. The implication is that the waters running out of the satisfied (full) lake will continue to flow into the abysmal ravine, until the once joyous lake is completely dry. A further image is of a tree that is fading because it is not allowed to spread its branches. It may be enclosed in such a way that it is being "straightened" against its natural tendency to bend; or it may simply be from lack of water, due to the drying up of the lake. Whatever the actual circumstances, the indication is that positive forces are feeling the repression of negative ones. The idea of something being straightened and distressed can be applied to a socio-political condition where the order and good government that would benefit the organization are temporarily being stifled. When the superior person meets such a situation, he remains master of himself, and pursues the proper course, according to his own inner voice. He accepts that the sacrifice will be great, and understands clearly that action is needed now—not words.

The image is of a dried-up lake, and the difficulties that the remaining trees must overcome.

THE LINES

1 | Avoid the trap of increasing distress by sinking into states of depression. Inner feelings of inadequacy must be overcome.

2 | The strengthening of spiritual practice will help one to overcome the feelings of inner oppression which lead to exhaustion. Be patient.

3 | One will pay a price for reckless, insensitive actions. Recognize the soft, peaceful way as the source of joy and inspiration.

4 | The lure of material rewards tempt one to compromise one's own inner truth. The condition is temporary. Further clarity is needed.

5 | One finds oneself alone, with no apparent help from above or below. Accept the situation gracefully, and joy will gradually return.

6 | One represses oneself by being over-cautious when the time to act has come. One must forgive oneself for past mistakes, and move on.

WELL

WELL is the symbol of source. It is comprised of the trigram water, positioned over that of wood, which gives the impression of a bucket being drawn up, full of water, for the nourishment of all. It is also represented by a plant, which draws the water upward through its roots to give life and sustenance to all that grows above the earth. This reminds us that the water drawn from the well should not only serve to quench the thirst of the thirsty, but must also be used to irrigate the crops for all the people. The superior person recognizes the significance of this symbolism, and conducts himself in such a manner that stimulates others to mutual helpfulness. The well itself, as a source of nourishment, remains consistent throughout whatever changes may take place in the socio-political organizations of the time. In ancient times, the well was always known to be the joint property of all the inhabitants of an area. Use was restricted only by the good intentions of all who drew from it. Even today, the well still represents a sure source of refreshment: the meeting-place where people go to fill their buckets with water from the cool depths of the earth. One must guard oneself against drinking from a polluted well, and pay careful attention to the maintenance of both bucket and rope. The inner walls of the well are likened to the depths of one's own inner

nature, and will support the physical structure so long as they are properly maintained.

The image is of water being drawn from the depths of the earth to nourish all things that exist on it.

5

THE LINES

1 | The well has not been maintained. Its muddy, disused state is reflected in the corrupt, useless and unregarded people who have not maintained their own inner development.

2 | The well is strong, but its cool waters cannot be brought to the top because the bucket is broken. Find more reliable helpers.

3 | One's talents and abilities are not being recognized. When they are, everyone will benefit. One must wait.

4 | The cultivation of oneself is fundamental to the proper leadership of others. One must first develop one's own inner resources.

5 | The blessings that flow from the virtuous person are available to all. Drink up!

6 | In sincerity, there will be good fortune. The waters that flow from the pure source are truly inexhaustible.

REVOLUTION

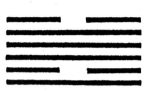

REVOLUTION is the symbol of change. The trigrams water and fire represent two elements whose natural forces oppose each other. In the hexagram Division we saw two forces whose tendencies were to move in opposite directions. In Revolution we are looking at something much more fundamental. Here the elements combat each other directly, rather than move apart; thus the more drastic action of revolutionary change is indicated. The changes called for are inevitable. Just as spring will give way to the fire of summer, so water will extinguish fire; and fire left to rage out of control will dry up water. Each of these elements produces a change in the other. The necessity for change is indisputably recognized. The hexagram Revolution addresses the spirit and manner under which it will most effectively be brought about. Since most people tend to view change, and especially major change, with suspicion and dislike, it is better not to try to implement things too quickly. Changes to socio-political organizations must be regulated by two fundamental conditions. There must be a proven necessity for the change beforehand, and it must be conducted with firm correctness that is free from all selfish motives.

The image is of fire within the lake, reflected in the ever changing seasons of time.

1 | One is advised to hold fast to the middle way, and not attempt to change too much too soon.

2 | Seek guidance from one whose inner light is brilliantly clear; and then proceed on your own intelligence. Action taken will be fortunate, and there will be no error.

3 | Avoid excesses of any nature. Extreme conservatism paralyzes; reckless and violent change will not succeed. Act cautiously, after due deliberation.

4 | One has earned the confidence needed to implement radical changes. Keep a broad view, and do not succumb to pettiness. Let harmony prevail.

5 | Bold action is indicated. Let everything be out in the open, for all to see that their trust has been well placed.

6 | The large changes are complete. Stay quiet, and let others complete their work.

CAULDRON

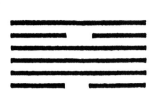

CAULDRON is the symbol of nourishment. With the trigram fire positioned over that of wood, we are introduced to the idea of a cooking vessel suspended over a fire. Two previous hexagrams, Nourishment and Well, deal with their own aspects of providing nourishment. Both are concerned with the physical nourishment of ordinary people, through agriculture or other methods. Cauldron and Well share a common factor in that they are the only two hexagrams named for things that are in everyday use by ordinary people. But the similarities stop here. The hexagram Cauldron is concerned with nourishing the spiritual aspects of man's higher self. The fact that it is expressed through the idea of a cooking vessel and fire is no mistake. This is designed to remind us of the harmony that must exist between the highest spiritual values, and the most ordinary activities of cooking and serving food. In ancient times, the cauldron was used as a ceremonial vessel to hold food for sacred rites and banquets of the highest order. It was also used to cook the family's food. What better way to get the point across that man is the ultimate expression of the divine? Enlightenment is experienced as the true understanding of the ways of heaven and earth.

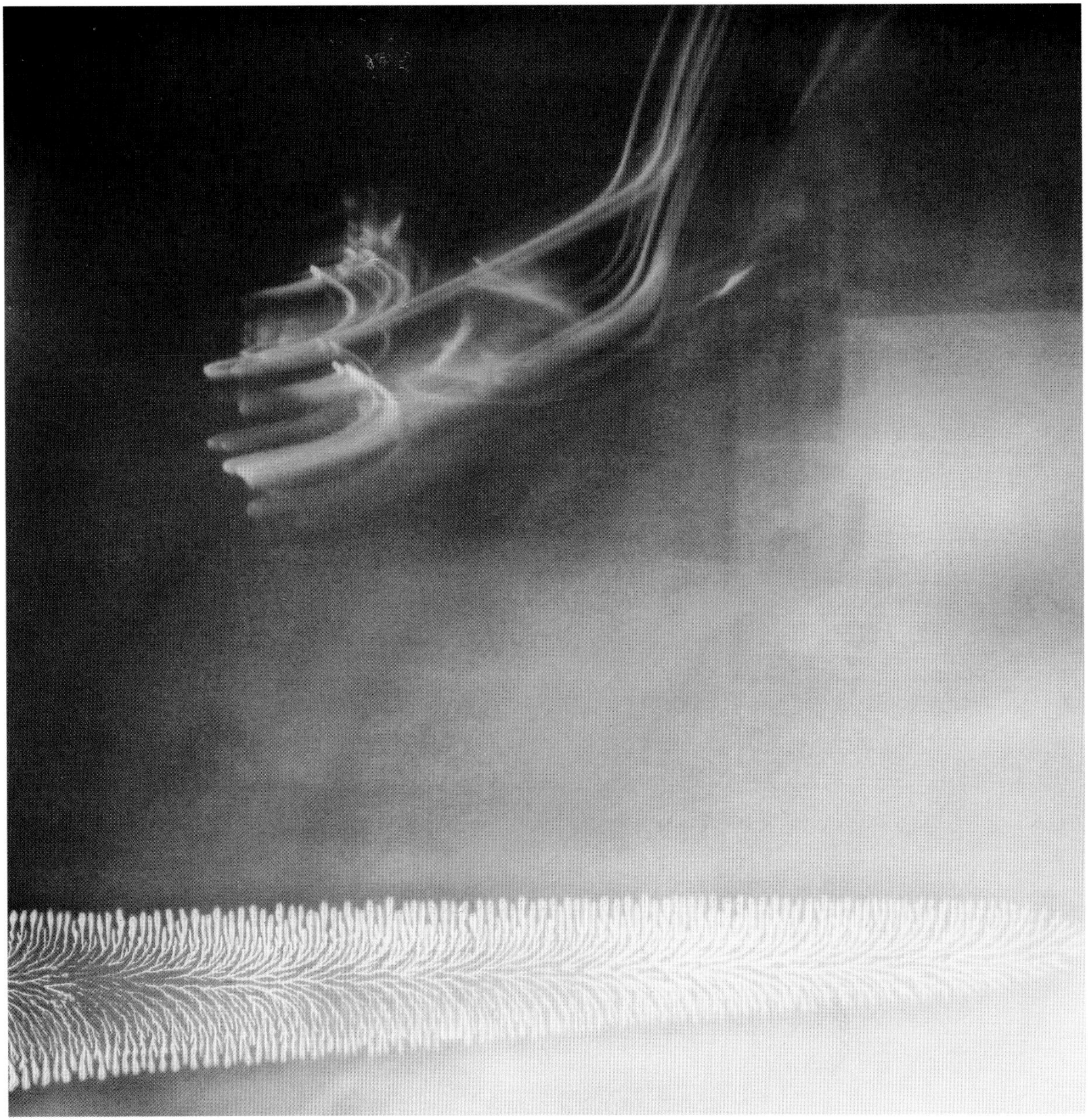

The image is of wood combining with fire, to cook the food in the sacred cauldron.

THE LINES

1 | One must empty oneself of what has been unnecessarily accumulated. Self-purification is the first step towards spiritual development.

2 | One must remain above reproach in all one's actions. If envy arises in someone else, make sure that it is not directed at you.

3 | One's gifts and talents may not be recognized or rewarded on the material level; but their spiritual worth is never denied.

4 | If a person is not able to progress by himself, he must seek reliable guidance. Otherwise, he must be prepared to accept the full responsibility of failure.

5 | Remember the middle way. Strong and able helpers will come to one who is receptive, approachable and modest; while at the same time, remaining firm and correct.

6 | Be like the jade, which, though its surface is hard, has a peculiar, rich softness of its own.

SHOCK

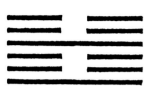

SHOCK is the symbol of moving, exciting power. The doubling of the trigram thunder signifies the arousing crash or peal. Symbolically, Shock indicates movement that is taking place in any type of organization, be it natural, social or purely personal. The purpose of the hexagram is to address the conduct to be pursued in a time of movement, particularly that of insurrection or revolution, by the people who are promoting, and most interested in, the situation. One is advised to be aware of the dangers of the time; and is shown how, by taking necessary precautions and regulating oneself, one will be able to overcome these dangers. The indication is that there will be success in moving and advancing—when the time is right. The power of Shock, reflected in thunder, is known to terrify and completely disorientate some people. Others perceive it as a stimulating force—a power that calls them to life anew, possibly after a particularly low period in their life. Some may even view it as an indication of a "second chance." Still others simply accept it as natural, as just one of nature's many wondrous ways of announcing change. When the movement, or crash of thunder, terrifies those all around, the superior person will not be shaken from his firm foundation in his own inner truth. He is aware of the danger, yet remains confident and self-possessed.

The image is of thunder upon thunder, pealing through the heavens, signaling a grand reawakening.

THE LINES

1 | Good fortune for one who is able to overcome his initial apprehensions. Later he will be seen smiling and talking cheerfully.

2 | One is in danger of losing everything. Let go of the material things, and preserve your inner worth. Balance will be restored .

3 | One feels distraught by the movements going on around one. Do not hesitate to take right action. Act with authenticity.

4 | Great effort will be needed to avoid the trap of a muddled mind, otherwise one will suffer from overwhelming inertia.

5 | The times are particularly dangerous, but if a person maintains his inner strength he will find the business that he can accomplish.

6 | One must take precautions to preserve one's own inner clarity. Withdraw at once, even from friends and family if necessary.

KEEPING STILL

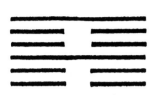

KEEPING STILL is the symbol of stability. It is made up of the trigram mountain positioned both on top and below. The significance of the repetition is found in the dual attributes of the mountain. In its active phase, it rises grandly from the surface of the earth, and then rests on itself in quiet and solemn majesty. But to the traveler the mountain represents a passive obstacle that arrests his onward progress. Hence the hexagram Keeping Still is concerned with the twofold implications of resting and arresting. It is the simultaneous existence of these two forces that reminds us that the end of one movement is, in reality, the beginning of the next. For the sake of the hexagram, we are concerned not only with resting, but with resting in what is right in every different situation in which a man can be placed. The symbolisms for these situations are expressed through various parts of the human body. The emphasis for Keeping Still is placed on the back, which unlike the eyes, ears and mouth, has no opening to draw it to what is outside of itself. Its main function is simply to stand straight and strong. So does the superior person rest in principle, free from the intrusion of selfish thoughts and external objects. He is not, however, a recluse, who keeps aloof from social commitments. His distinction is that he maintains his firm inner composure, both when he is alone and when he is mingling with others.

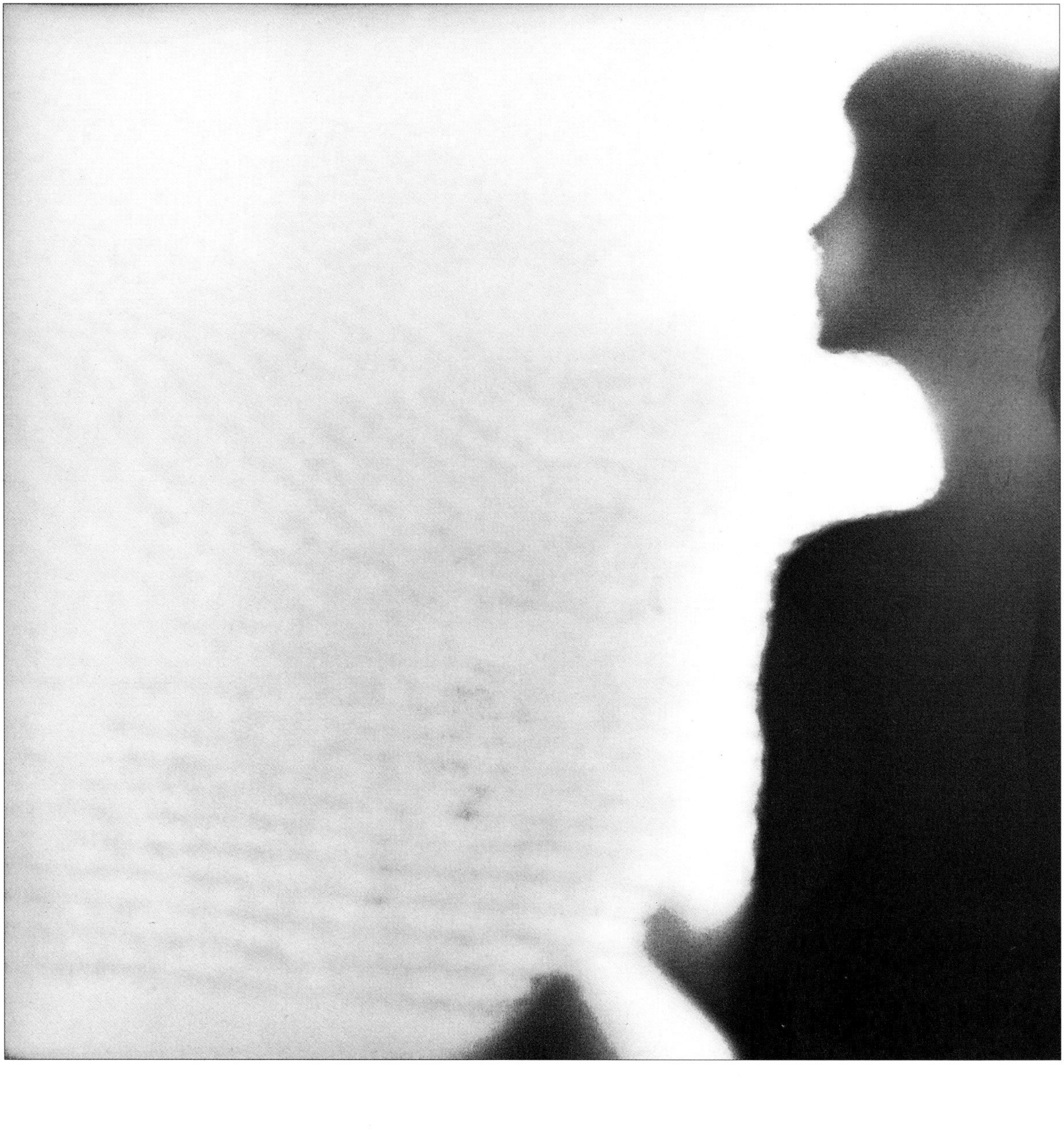

The image is of a majestic mountain, resting and arresting by its very nature.

THE LINES

1 | So long as one is persistently firm and correct, there will be no error in action, or in non-action.

2 | A person can save himself from the path of wrongdoing, but cannot force another to follow suit, especially one whose wrong path he has previously followed.

3 | Forced rigidity will lead to isolation, not meditation. True discipline rises from within; it is not repressively imposed.

4 | One whose body is peacefully at rest will be free from agitation.

5 | A superior person's words will reflect his harmonious inner nature. Avoid idle chatter.

6 | Let the peaceful stillness that has developed within extend naturally to every outward action.

PROGRESSIVE ADVANCE

PROGRESSIVE ADVANCE is the symbol of gradual progress. The positioning of the trigram wood, with its attribute of flexible penetration, over that of the restful mountain, indicates an onward movement that is inexhaustible; it will go on for an indefinite time, and then be succeeded by rest again. The theme of advance has already been addressed in two previous hexagrams, each of which has its own peculiarity of meaning. Progressive Advance deals most directly with the gradual manner in which the advance takes place. It outlines the successive steps that one must take gradually, under various conditions that lead to positions of influence in the community. Attention is drawn to the careful preliminary steps that must be continued all the way through any important event, from its initiation to its consummation. All must be done in an orderly and correct manner. The image of a tree growing strong on a mountain side is used to illustrate the gradualness of the progress. Every morning and every evening shows some difference in the size of the branches. When the tree has reached its maturity, whether it be of ordinary or extraordinary size, it will have taken years to reach its present dimensions. The superior person understands that the maintenance of virtue and the improvement of manners are gradual processes.

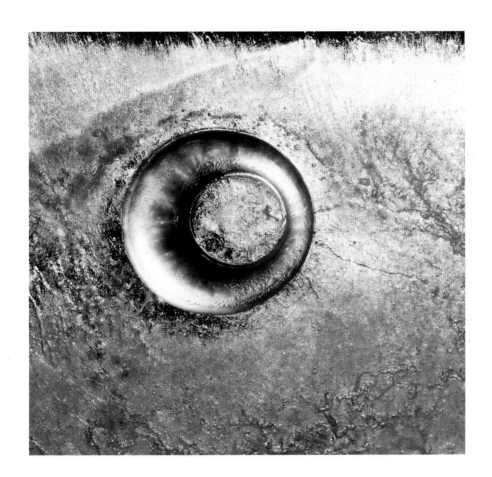

The image is of a tree, high upon a mountain side, spreading its roots into the earth and its branches into the sky for all to see.

THE LINES

1 | One is about to embark on a new adventure. Surrounded by danger, it is wise to hesitate. Progress gradually, and there will be no error.

2 | Follow the example of the wild goose, and invite friends to share in your good fortune. Confidence is built slowly.

3 | One must not allow oneself to advance too far, too quickly; especially in a hostile place. Any sign of arrogance or selfishness will bring trouble.

4 | The situation is dangerous, and the territory unfamiliar. Seek a temporary resting-place.

5 | One's actions are misunderstood, and one's efforts misjudged. Don't despair. The misunderstandings will be resolved, and good fortune will result.

6 | One's work is complete. Stand firm, and be recognized as an example to others.

MARRYING MAIDEN

MARRYING MAIDEN is the symbol of love. The trigram of thunder, representing the arousing, positioned over that of the lake, indicates a joyous woman who gladly rises up to follow the man of her choice. This hexagram offers a person the opportunity to broaden his understanding of the powerful union of heaven and earth, that in this case is represented in the loving relationships that develop between individuals. It is concerned with the voluntary relations that exist between east and west, spring and autumn, and man and woman. Everyone who enters a new family or relationship must do so with great care and respect for the present members. Where traditions and accepted codes of behavior are already established, one must make every effort to comply with them. If one is unable to submit willingly to the demands of the union, it is better to withdraw at the onset, rather than conduct oneself dishonestly. True union depends on love. Legally regulated relationships can be governed by arbitrary rules based on rights and duties; but relationships based on personal inclinations will depend on the love and consideration that each party shows for the other. The superior person understands that spontaneous affection is the strong bond in meaningful relations.

The image is of the arousing thunder, stirring the cool and joyous waters of the lake.

1 | A person must conduct himself tactfully in all situations, particularly those in which he feels to be "out of position."

2 | Two people who devote themselves in a responsible fashion to each other will accomplish things that neither would be able to do alone.

3 | One who knowingly enters into a relationship just to avoid being alone, risks losing his self-esteem.

4 | One may need to wait a long time for the right person to present himself. Inappropriate liaisons must be avoided. The wait will be worth while.

5 | If one is free from vanity, one will be able to adapt without difficulty to any social condition. Be humble.

6 | Do not be coerced into a union that is shallow or superficial. Such irreverence will not benefit anyone.

ABUNDANCE

ABUNDANCE is the symbol of prosperity. The trigram thunder positioned over that of fire denotes a condition of abundant prosperity, fueled by intelligence within and manifested through the motive force without. In the course of human affairs, as in nature, one is reminded that a condition of prosperity will eventually give place to one of an opposite character. The hexagram Abundance shows one how to gain the most benefit from this time of prosperity. The figure intimates progress and development. A person is advised not to be anxious, but to study how he can develop himself to the point where his inner nature shines like the sun at its zenith. He must make every effort to avoid complacency, and to be temperate in all actions. The energetic clarity with which he can now tackle any obstacle can be likened to the flash of lightning that rises so naturally to the call of thunder. In the hexagram Biting Through, we saw the same trigrams of fire and thunder, but there their positions were more relevant to the fair and just administration of punishments. Now, as we see lightning joined with thunder as different but equal properties, we witness a force that is capable of cheering and enlightening all the people.

The image is of thunder and lightning, coming together in a brilliant display.

1 | One is encouraged to go forward with a like-minded partner. Mutual helpfulness is the great instrument for the maintenance of prosperity—even if it does not last for ever.

2 | It will not be acceptable to advance right now. One is viewed with suspicion and dislike. The only recourse is to go inside and develop one's own inner light.

3 | When a person has no one to co-operate with, he must accept that matters are beyond his control, and concentrate on his own capacity for goodness to save himself from error.

4 | After a period of extreme darkness, a person meets his devoted partner again. There will be good fortune.

5 | At last, those people of brilliant ability begin to move forward together. This is a time for rejoicing and congratulations. Nothing consolidates prosperity like co-operation.

6 | A person must be careful not to isolate himself through arrogance, especially at the pinnacle of success. Be humble.

WANDERER

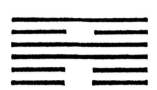

WANDERER is the symbol of wandering or seeking. The positioning of the trigram fire over that of the mountain reflects the influence of intelligence on quiet restfulness. The implication is that if the stranger, or traveller, be firm and correct as he ought to be, there will be good fortune. The two main qualities that must be developed are humbleness and integrity. A person must restrain himself from becoming overbearing or arrogant, and remain cautious and reserved. In this way he will escape harm, and can expect to make some degree of progress. One who is reserved and unpretentious cannot be humiliated, even if he is in a strange situation. The wanderer's lot is such that he has no fixed abode. He makes his home as he travels the road. Therefore he must select his destinations carefully, and travel only in the right direction, with the right people. Only then will he be assured of making his way unmolested, and without bringing misfortune to himself and others. In the hexagram Wanderer, one is reminded that fire burns quickly off the face of the mountain; it does not linger. In the same manner, one is encouraged to exert wisdom and caution in the use of punishments, and not allow lawsuits and penalties to be prolonged.

The image is of a fire burning quickly on the face of a mountain; bright without, yet calm and reserved within.

THE LINES

1 | One's position is vulnerable, and will only be worsened if one allows oneself to become involved with trivial and unworthy people.

2 | By developing his own inner being, a person will be provided with everything he can possibly require. On this trust, faithful friendships are formed.

3 | A person who interferes in matters that are none of his business will soon find himself alone and unsupported.

4 | Finding a resting-place does not mean that one can become complacent. Be prepared to defend yourself, and continue the search for inner peace.

5 | One endears oneself to others by showing respect for their customs and traditions. Even among strangers, one will find friends.

6 | One must guard against any signs of arrogance or imprudent conduct. Violence will not be tolerated.

MILDNESS

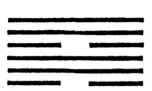

MILDNESS is the symbol of penetration. The doubling of the trigram wind indicates a gentleness or adaptability that is able to penetrate everywhere, even into dark or unconscious places. In nature, we see that the wind is able to disperse the dark clouds, and return the sky to its clear state. In the human condition, it is the penetrating clarity of discrimination that enables one to dispel the darkness of negativity. A person must be prepared to accept the guidance offered by one who is wiser and more experienced, just as the grasses bend in gentle compliance to the force of the wind. This flexible, harmonious attitude will be of great benefit when he finds himself in difficult situations. Penetration is able to effect its changes without violence; but rather through subtle, persistent influence that reaches everywhere. One may feel as though nothing extraordinary is happening. This is absolutely true. The great work that takes place in the inner world is very often not manifested immediately in the outer world. The effects of such work, however, are much more enduring and complete than those brought on by brute force. The superior person is acutely aware of the penetrating power of his influence, and thus makes sure that his every action is the sincere expression of his own, unclouded inner truth.

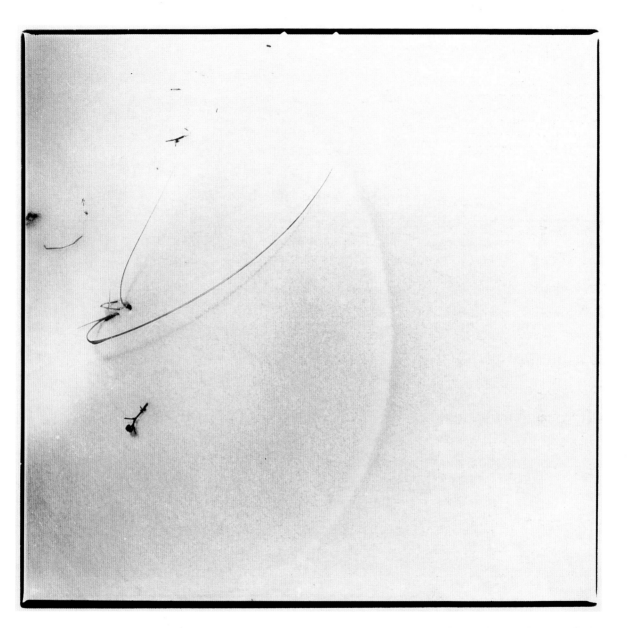

The image is of wind blowing gently over wind, bringing the possibility of enlightenment to all.

THE LINES

1 | Indecisiveness reflects the mental difficulties that arise when one has lost confidence in one's own inner voice.

2 | A person must find the courage to uncover his own deep-seated fears, which may appear to be blocking his forward progress. Openness and honesty will help.

3 | Excessive determination will lead to violence, just as prolonged vacillation will lead to exhaustion. Make a decision, and then act on it.

4 | One must not lose sight of practical matters in order to pursue spiritual ones. The superior person maintains a proper balance.

5 | What may appear to be a bad beginning can come to a favorable conclusion if one remains correct and firm, and therefore free from guilt.

6 | If one exceeds the limits of due measure, and attempts to explore dangerous regions without proper guidance and protection, one must be prepared to suffer the consequences.

JOY

JOY is the symbol of pleased satisfaction. The doubling of the trigram water, depicted as the joining of two lakes, indicates the way in which joy, wisdom and experience are all reinforced when shared among like-minded people. Each of the trigrams is comprised of two yang (strong) lines at the bottom, representing firm correctness, and one yin (weak) line above, representing yielding gentleness. This arrangement is in accord with the natural order of the universe. The effect of doubling this trigram of water is to indicate how the superior person, whose joy emanates from his own inner truth, will be able to stimulate the people to overcome their barriers and themselves proceed with joy. The joyous mood is infectious, in the most positive sense, and therefore capable of inspiring people to encourage one another in their efforts. Tasks that previously appeared to be tiresome and arduous are transformed through a joyous attitude. The advantage of having two lakes (or people) is that they will replenish each other, and therefore neither one will dry up so quickly. This is especially advantageous when one is seeking to increase one's knowledge, whether it be spiritual or practical. The superior person will joyfully encourage stimulating conversation among friends, and gently guide them in their common practices.

The image is of two lakes replenishing each other, as the superior person studies and practices with his friends.

1 | The good fortune attached to the pleasure of inward harmony arises from there being nothing in one's conduct to induce doubt.

2 | The pleasure that arises from inward sincerity is due to the confidence that one has in one's own inner truth. This will bring respect.

3 | One who indulges in excessive, indiscriminate pursuits of physical pleasure will find himself in a spiritual wasteland.

4 | One cannot be truly at rest while deliberating about which path of pleasure to pursue. Choose the higher, and then get on with it.

5 | One is advised to move cautiously in dangerous situations. Unfortunately, some people are not yet worthy of trust, and therefore should be avoided.

6 | If a person loses touch with his own inner truth, he will easily be seduced by the superficial pleasures of leading and attracting others. Be aware.

DISSOLUTION

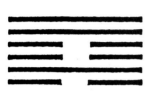

DISSOLUTION is the symbol of dispersion. The position of the trigram wind over that of the abysmal water indicates a situation where water is dispersed by the moving wind. This is the same gentle wind that we saw doubled in the hexagram Mildness, not a raging tornado. It dissipates the dark clouds of unconsciousness by penetrating to the very source of the problem, and then remaining correct and firm. Dissolution is concerned with the condition that results when people's minds are alienated from what is right and good. Left unattended, this state would surely lead to disorder and eventual disunity. The hexagram Dissolution shows how the situation can be dealt with and remedied, by persistently dissolving the blockages. The indication is that under these conditions there will be progress and success. The superior person recognizes the need to call on the spirits of his ancestors for guidance, and sees clearly that the temple is the place of union. The celebration of great religious feasts and sacred rites of all traditions will do much to enhance social unity. One must guard against the rigidity that is born out of hardness and selfish tendencies, and carry out all actions with due regard for what is right.

The image is of the gentle wind, that is able to penetrate even the rigidity of ice, and start it flowing again.

THE LINES

1 | One has the opportunity to disperse misunderstandings before their influence becomes widespread, if one is prepared to take quick and vigorous action.

2 | One has created an inner sanctuary for oneself. Do not allow this to turn into an isolation tank. One should examine oneself carefully, and remove any signs of hatred or ill-will immediately.

3 | A person who can set aside all personal desires, and strive for a goal outside himself, will recognize the true workings of dispersion.

4 | The superior person understands that dispersion leads to accumulation, and gathers round him those good people who have been set adrift.

5 | At the height of dispersion, people respond favorably to a brilliant new idea that is set forth honestly and with conviction.

6 | A person must decide for himself if the dangers are too great, and if so remove himself and his family at once.

REGULATION

REGULATION is the symbol of regulated restriction. The positioning of the two trigrams that represent various aspects of water—the abysmal over that of the lake—indicates the way in which natural limitations actually strengthen the social order. Without some form of restriction, the lake, if continually supplied with more and more water, will overflow its banks and be diminished. In social conditions, the abysmal water may be seen as the regulating factor that prevents the joyousness of the lake from spilling over into hysterical, unconscious frivolity. The analogy is also drawn to indicate the joints that give stability and flexibility to a stem of bamboo, in much the same way as the joints function in the human body, and the seasons of the year are regulated in an orderly fashion. The hexagram indicates that under these conditions there will be progress and attainment. Although the tasks to be undertaken may be quite dangerous, they will be directed by one's feeling of pleasure and satisfaction. When regulations are set and maintained in accordance with the laws of heaven, the superior person will recognize his freedom, and all actions will proceed from this correct position. Self-limitation is the basis of freedom.

The image is of nature, regulating the flow of water both into and out of the lake.

THE LINES

1 | Great discrimination is needed, in words as well as in actions. Do not attempt to go forward, and exercise a cautious judgement in all matters.

2 | After careful consideration, the time has come to act. To hesitate, now that the obstacles have been removed, would bring misfortune.

3 | One who shows no appearance of observing the proper regulations will come to regret his foolish extravagances. Freedom comes to one who corrects his errors.

4 | Avoid unnecessary struggles. Maintain a quiet and natural attention to proper regulations, and inner strength will be replenished.

5 | A person must not attempt to put restrictions on others that he is not prepared to comply with himself. By his own good example he will gain the co-operation of others.

6 | Excessively severe restrictions will not endure. One who attempts to enforce them will not succeed.

CENTRAL SINCERITY

CENTRAL SINCERITY is the symbol of inner truth. The trigram wind positioned over that of water allows us to see the visible effects of an invisible force. The hexagram is composed of two yin (weak) lines resting in the innermost part of the figure, supported at the top and bottom by two strong (yang) lines in their central places. The attributes of flexible penetration and pleased satisfaction represented by the trigrams indicate that sincerity, thus placed, will be able to transform the individual and, therefore, nations. The idea of innermost sincerity clearly states that one must develop one's own inner truth before its influence will be able to spread to those who appear to be unreachable. Only when a person rids himself of all prejudice will he be able to understand the mind and heart of another. From this mutual understanding, relationships will develop where the influence of one gently penetrates the will of the other, without any sign of restraint. The superior person will call on this same deep understanding to penetrate the minds and hearts of others, when he may be called upon to pass judgements on their mistakes. His careful deliberations will spring from a crystal clarity, guided by his own sympathetic appreciation of the circumstances. Forgiveness is founded on a strong base of central sincerity.

The image is of the wind on the lake, gently penetrating the minds and hearts of all the people.

THE LINES

1 | One is presently resting in one's own inner truth. Trust that this is the right place to be, and stop looking for outside influences.

2 | A responsive heart recognizes the call of another responsive heart, and the circle grows wider and wider of its own accord.

3 | One must be careful not to become dependent on others. Maintain inner sincerity, and thus avoid unwarranted feelings of uncertainty.

4 | One may need to separate oneself from the others for a while to strengthen one's inner development. Seek inspiration of a spiritual nature.

5 | When a person is perfectly sincere, others will be linked with him through their own inner truth. Bonds formed through inner sincerity will endure.

6 | Beware of vanity. Remain modest and humble to avoid misfortune.

SMALL EXCESS

SMALL EXCESS is the symbol of minor preponderance. The trigram thunder, positioned over that of the mountain, suggests a time of keeping still out of necessity. To attempt to move bullishly forward in such overpowering circumstances would be disastrous. We are reminded of the hexagram Large Excess, which prepared us for extraordinary undertakings during extraordinary times. Now we have another exceptional situation, one that will require great restraint and humbleness. There will be progress and attainment, but only in small affairs, not great ones. It will be advantageous to remain firm and correct, for without these qualities one exposes oneself to the threat of great misfortune. When one needs to distinguish the essential from the non-essential, and considers whether it is ever beneficial to deviate from the prescribed course of action, the answer is "no"— not in the matter of what is right. In small matters of a non-essential nature, deviations may be made, and can be expected to produce favorable results. But one must make these changes very carefully, with great humbleness and reverence. Even in times of transition, one may give up one's recognized form of practice; but never the substance of inner truth.

The image is of thunder on the mountain, reminding one of the importance of a humble nature.

THE LINES

1 | When a person is obsessed with the idea of exceeding the limits of the situation, he places himself in great danger. This is the time to keep still.

2 | The requirements of the time cannot make wrong right, or right wrong. But they can modify the conventional course of action to be taken.

3 | One must not become too confident in one's own strength, and fail to take necessary precautions against hidden dangers.

4 | Resist the temptation to go forward forcefully. One is warned to move quietly and with restraint.

5 | The time of transition is very near, but one is unable to ascend without the support of able helpers. Choose them carefully.

6 | When a person refuses to keep himself under restraint, and presses on out of control, he will have to accept that his injury, and the resultant calamity, are self-produced.

COMPLETION

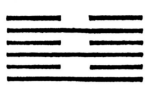

COMPLETION is the symbol of successful accomplishment. With the positioning of the trigram abysmal water over that of fire, we see two elements occupying their proper places. The two forces are, by their natures, opposed to one another, and as we saw in the hexagram Revolution, sometimes they combat each other directly. Completion, however, represents the condition of successful accomplishment, when, after a long and difficult period, it is finally time to rest and remain quiet. The transition from the chaos to the calm has already been accomplished, the distresses have been relieved, and the disorders returned to order. Everything is in its proper place. Now the changes must be consolidated into daily life. The balanced interaction of these two opposing elements will be beneficial, and in small matters there will be progress and success. One is reminded that it is precisely when things are in their proper order that one needs to pay careful attention to details. The superior person understands the nature of the supreme force that regulates the changing of the seasons; and he recognizes the implications of its influence in his own socio-political situations. Great understanding arises when he realizes that same force as his own inner truth, and proceeds cautiously, fully aware of the instability of all human affairs.

The image is of the alchemical change that occurs when water is transformed by the heat of fire into steam.

THE LINES

1 | One has earned this time of rest, and must be sensible enough to take it. Do not be swayed by the opinions of others or the excitement of the times.

2 | Success has been achieved. Wait patiently through this time of transition. One is advised to keep oneself quietly hidden, thus ready for action when it will again be required.

3 | Expansion for the sake of expansion will drain one of valuable resources. Do not employ inferior people to perform unnecessary tasks. Danger lurks.

4 | One must take every precaution not to expose oneself to harmful influences. Intuition is a powerful ally—trust it.

5 | One whose small contributions are offered sincerely will receive great blessings. Avoid pretentious situations that do not touch your heart.

6 | Once the danger has been passed, be careful not to dwell on it, or to gloat over your success in surpassing it.

BEFORE COMPLETION

BEFORE COMPLETION is the symbol of what is not yet completed. The trigram fire positioned over that of the abysmal water indicates a situation where the two elements cannot act on each other. It is the nature of fire to ascend, and that of water to descend. The symbolism is thus interpreted to represent the unregulated condition of general affairs that exists when people are unable to act in harmony with each other. The yin and yang lines are arranged exactly opposite to the natural order in which they appear in the previous hexagram Completion. The ordering of the lines in Before Completion does, however, offer each of the lines in the lower trigram its proper corresponding line in the upper one. This rather extended method of balancing indicates that, although successful accomplishment has not yet been attained, there is some successful progress to be made. The pervading theme of Before Completion is that there is no such thing as a perfectly constant, abiding state. All things will change, just as the seasons do. In this particular condition of Before Completion, one is presented with the situation where the reign of order has been experienced. Now it has terminated, and the hexagram calls to the superior person to see to it that the struggle for its realization is begun anew. It suggests how one who is engaged in that struggle will conduct himself, with a view to securing his joyful fulfillment.

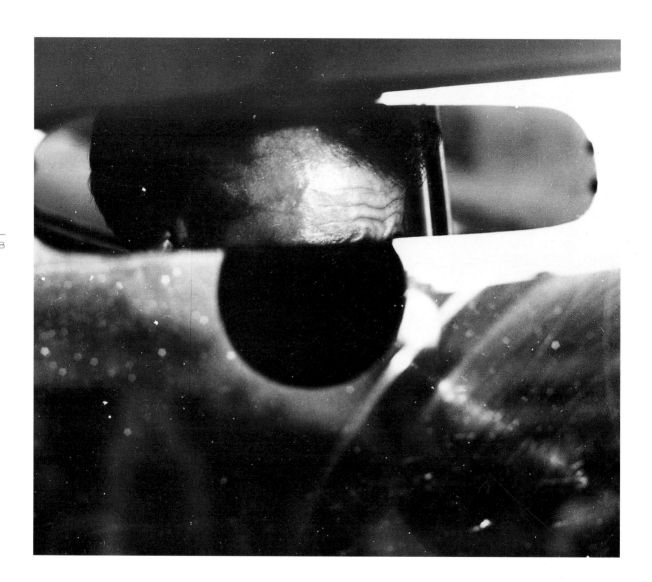

The image is of the independent natures of fire and water, reflected in the transitional period of spring.

THE LINES

1 | The situation, as it now stands, is beyond repair. By advancing unconsciously, one only invites further danger and trouble.

2 | A person is advised to wait patiently, and develop his own inner strength. Then, when the time is right, his actions will bring good fortune.

3 | One is already in the midst of transition, and will not be able to succeed unassisted. Select helpers carefully; and rely on your own inner truth.

4 | Now the time to act has come. The task is indeed great; for as a person overcomes the present difficulties, he lays the groundwork for what is to come.

5 | The superior person remains humble, even in victory; and thus his influence is far-reaching.

6 | One's diligent efforts are rewarded. Enjoy the celebration—just remember the middle way.

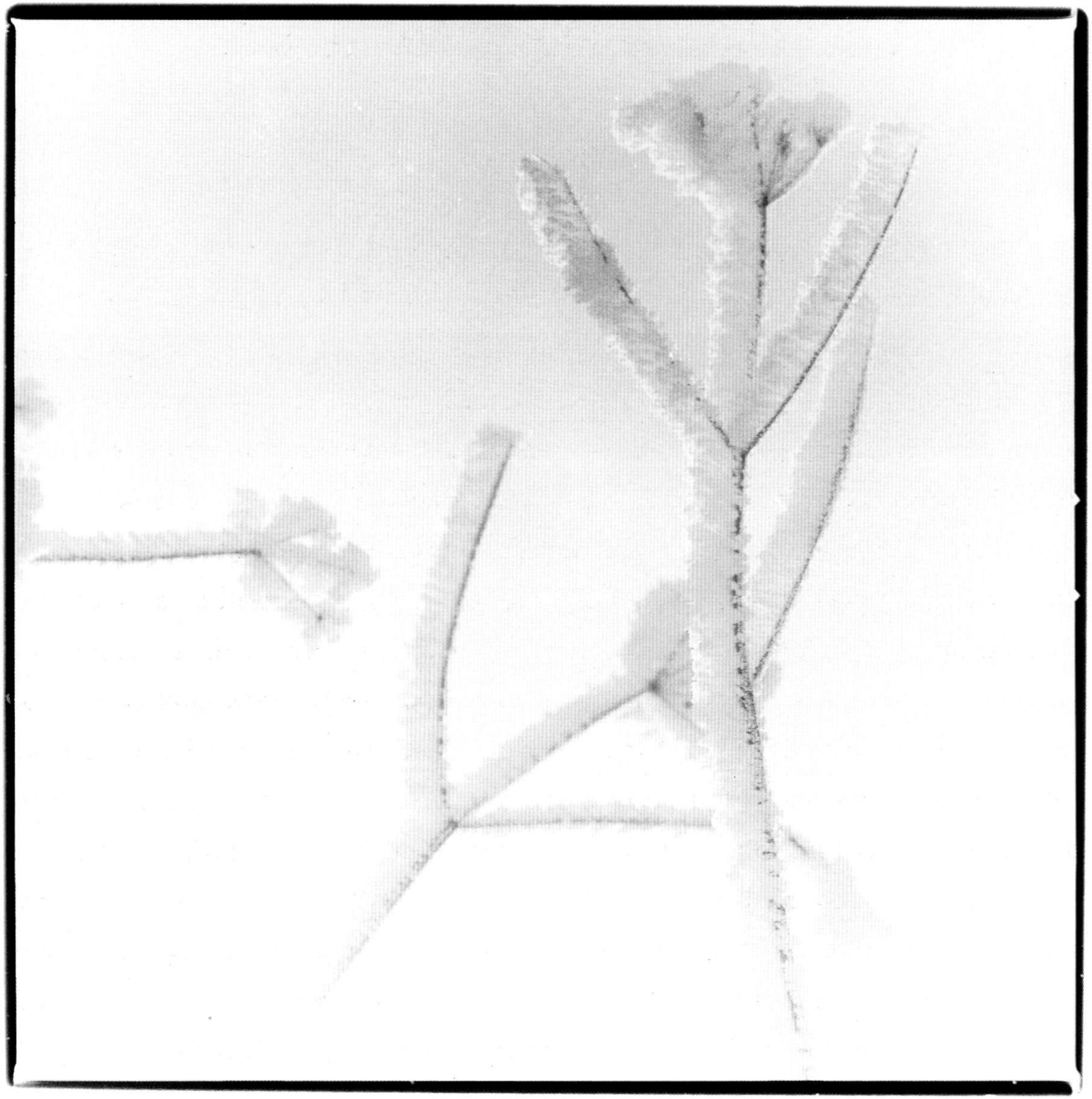

Consulting the Oracle

THE *I CHING* has been interpreted, throughout the ages, in a variety of ways. Some people view this extraordinary work more as an inspirational companion than a means of fortune telling. James Legge, whose scholarly translation of the ancient Chinese text is the source for this edition, included no instructions on how to consult the oracle. Other people are more interested in applying the timeless wisdom contained within the sixty-four hexagrams to their own personal situations. For those of us who appreciate the remarkable divinatory qualities of the *I Ching,* whether applied personally or generally, the following pages outline a method of consultation that involves the tossing of three identically marked coins. This particular method has been selected because it is much less complicated than using yarrow stalks. The very fact that it relies on the vagaries of chance challenges the analytical, Western mind to relax its demand for control. If we are going to do something so unscientific as to toss coins, then we must be willing to accept that the element of chance reflected in their fall will represent an integral part of the outcome. The act of tossing the coins itself requires the same degree of reverence and respect that we give to any other form of divination. In making the decision to consult the *I Ching,* we are simply opening ourselves to this marvellous flow of universal wisdom.

The purpose of tossing the coins is to determine the nature of each of the six

Ch'ien	Heaven, the Sky	Untiring strength; power	The creative
Chen	Thunder	Moving; exciting power	The arousing
K'an	Water, Rain or Clouds, the Moon	Peril; difficulty; dangerous	The abysmal
Ken	Mountain, or Hills	Resting; the act of arresting; firm; quiet	Keeping still
K'un	The Earth	Capaciousness; submission; devotion; yielding	The receptive
Sun	The Wind, or Wood	Flexibility; penetrating; enduring	The gentle
Li	Fire, Lightning, the Sun	Brightness; elegance; clarity	The clinging
Tui	Water, collected in a Lake	Pleasure; complacent satisfaction; joy	The joyous

THE TRIGRAMS

lines that comprise each hexagram. According to Chinese philosophy, everything in existence is composed of a particular balance of the two primal forces of yin and yang. Yang refers to energy that is creative and active. Yin is receptive and passive. The interaction of these two forces regulates everything that exists in the universe. The individual lines of the hexagrams are created according to their balance of yin and yang elements.

By assigning a yin side and a yang side to each coin, and tossing the coins six times in succession, one can record the appearances of yin and yang and relate the resulting diagram to one of the sixty-four hexagrams. The easiest way to do this is to give the numerical value of two to that side of the coin that you decide reflects the yin principle, and that of three to the one that represents the yang. If you are using modern coins inscribed with a monetary value instead of Chinese characters, you might wish to expand your interpretation of the yin and yang elements to suit the particular coins that you have selected.

The different combinations of values shown when the coins are tossed are recorded in the following manner when making a consultation:

2 + 2 + 2 = 6	(*3 yin*) Moving yin line	—x—
2 + 2 + 3 = 7	(*2 yin, 1 yang*) Yang (or unbroken) line	———
3 + 3 + 2 = 8	(*2 yang, 1 yin*) Yin (or broken) line	– –
3 + 3 + 3 = 9	(*3 yang*) Moving yang line	—o—

The significance of a moving line is that, as in nature, when it has reached its peak it will begin to change into its polar opposite. The "x" and "o" on the lines shown above are only there to remind you that these are moving lines—which you will be changing to make a second hexagram.

Now hold the coins in your hands for a few moments, and open yourself to the great source of wisdom that you are about to consult. Consider the subject on which you would like to receive guidance from the *I Ching*. The nature of the question itself determines how much benefit we will be able to draw from the response. Formulate your question in such a way that you will not be asking for a simple yes or no answer. The timeless wisdom of the *I Ching* applies to every aspect of our being. Even when we ask a question on a very particular issue, we will still receive information that may speak to us on many other levels. Writing the question down at the beginning of the consultation is a good way to focus your attention on it.

Shake the coins, and release them on to a flat surface. Referring to the table above, observe the combination of coins before you, and record the line which corresponds to it. This first line forms the bottom line of the hexagram.

Then collect the coins in your hands, and shake them before casting them for a second time. Observe the combination, and draw a second line above the first. Repeat the process until you have completed six tosses of the coins. The resulting six lines will create the hexagram that contains the most relevant information to your particular question.

If there are any moving lines in the hexagram, draw a second hexagram beside it, in which any moving yang line in the original is now drawn as a yin line, and any moving yin line is drawn as a yang line. This resulting hexagram will add another dimension to your question.

Locate your first hexagram in the book, with the help of the diagram "Locating the hexagrams" on page 205. Read the commentary on the hexagram

UPPER TRIGRAM / LOWER TRIGRAM	Ch'ien ☰	Chen ☳	K'an ☵	Ken ☶	K'un ☷	Sun ☴	Li ☲	Tui ☱
Ch'ien ☰	1	34	5	26	11	9	14	43
Chen ☳	25	51	3	27	24	42	21	17
K'an ☵	6	40	29	4	7	59	64	47
Ken ☶	33	62	39	52	15	53	56	31
K'un ☷	12	16	8	23	2	20	35	45
Sun ☴	44	32	48	18	46	57	50	28
Li ☲	13	55	63	22	36	37	30	49
Tui ☱	10	54	60	41	19	61	38	58

LOCATING THE HEXAGRAMS

for a general reply to your question. Any moving lines signify those areas of your inquiry that require further attention. It is only for these moving, or changing, lines that the detailed information found in the sections designated as "The lines" has been added to the original text. Read the notes next to the numbers that correspond to the moving lines only, remembering that the lines are numbered from the bottom to the top. If you have drawn a second hexagram, only the body of the text relating to this hexagram will be pertinent, as the lines will not require any further clarification.

Take care to formulate your questions sincerely. If you treat the consultation as a parlor game, you will get a parlor game response. Remember that the *I Ching* is an ontological system—one that incorporates all aspects of "beingness." Any question that you put to the oracle may be answered from any number of different perspectives, and the insights that arise from consulting the *I Ching* may take a while to fully register in your being. You might find that you ask a question about one aspect of your life, and get an answer about something else that seems to be totally unrelated. This is as clear an indication that the system is working as that momentary spine-tingling clarity that you get when you feel that some one is reading your mind. This is precisely what happens when we consult the oracle. We are given the opportunity to read our own mind, without all the clouds and shadows of our restrictive conditioning. The wisdom that we attribute to the *I Ching* already lives in each and every one of us. Anything that we do to help reactivate our knowledge of it, and to reintegrate its practice into our daily lives, can only benefit ourselves and all other sentient beings. The simple act of tossing the coins could be the first step in that direction.

THE PHOTOGRAPHS

ACKNOWLEDGMENTS

The publishers and photographer would like to thank Roger Hammond for permission to use a detail of his photograph of the New York skyline (Hexagram 55), Henry Twinch for the use of his photograph of Mt Atitlan for Hexagram 41 and Sam Adams for assistance with printing the photograph of fire beech (Hexagram 49). Personal thanks also to Su Rose; Jane RR at Pulsynetic; and James Moores, whose independent support and encouragement made this publication possible.